MW01030643

DESTROYING THE
SPIRIT OF REJECTION

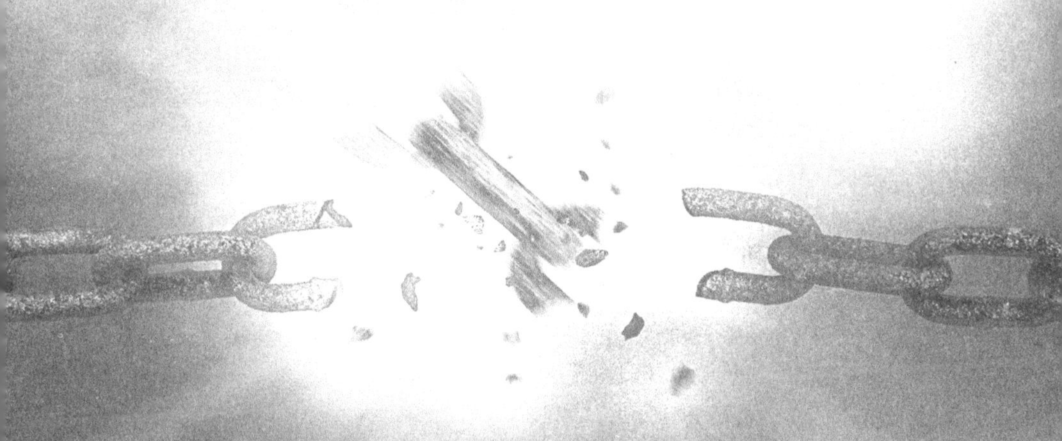

DESTROYING THE SPIRIT OF REJECTION

JOHN ECKHARDT

CHARISMA HOUSE

Most Charisma House Book Group products are available at special quantity discounts for bulk purchase for sales promotions, premiums, fund-raising, and educational needs. For details, write Charisma House Book Group, 600 Rinehart Road, Lake Mary, Florida 32746, or telephone (407) 333-0600.

Destroying the Spirit of Rejection by John Eckhardt
Published by Charisma House
Charisma Media/Charisma House Book Group
600 Rinehart Road
Lake Mary, Florida 32746
www.charismahouse.com

Design Director: Justin Evans

Visit the author's website at www.johneckhardtministries.com

Library of Congress Cataloging-in-Publication Data:
An application to register this book for cataloging has been submitted to the Library of Congress.
International Standard Book Number: 978-1-62998-770-5
E-book ISBN: 978-1-62998-771-2

While the author has made every effort to provide accurate telephone numbers and Internet addresses at the time of publication, neither the publisher nor the author assumes any responsibility for errors or for changes that occur after publication.

First edition

16 17 18 19 20 — 9 8 7 6 5 4 3 2 1
Printed in the United States of America

CONTENTS

INTRODUCTION

ROBBED AND SPOILED

But this is a people robbed and despoiled; they are all snared in holes, and they are hidden in prison houses; they are for a prey, and no one delivers, for a spoil, and no one says, "Restore them." Who among you will give ear to this? Who will listen and hear for the time to come?

—ISAIAH 42:22–23

REJECTION IS ONE of the most destructive demonic spirits to enter a person's life; it is a spoiler. One of the meanings of the verb *spoil* is "ruin." Therefore we see that rejection can ruin every life it encounters. The enemy uses rejection to rob people of their dignity, identity, position, power, and authority. Rejection wreaks havoc on people's lives, preventing them from experiencing the fullness and blessing of God.

Rejection can be as simple as being told no or being turned down for an opportunity we wanted. Rejection can escalate to being told we don't fit in or we don't belong. We experience rejection on a regular basis at these levels. We even reject things that don't work for us.

But the most damaging kind of rejection begins very early in life, many times through some kind of abuse, abandonment, or lack of love and affection from a parent. This type of rejection is common to many and sets us off on an unstable course in life that makes it difficult to handle any other rejection that we are sure to come in contact with. We try all kinds of ways to cover up rejection: people pleasing, attention seeking, perfectionism, anger and bitterness, hard-heartedness, pride, isolation, addiction to drugs or alcohol, and sexual promiscuity. We use any number of things to either gain love and acceptance or to protect ourselves from being hurt again. Rejection is a vicious cycle that takes us deeper and deeper into sin and destruction. After it does its damage, rejection leaves lives desolated and in ruins.

In Isaiah 42:22–23 the prophet Isaiah reveals the condition of the people of Israel after multiple attacks from surrounding enemies had left them desolated and in ruin. These verses also give a picture of what our lives are like after we have been raided and ravished by the enemy. Have you ever been robbed? If so, you know it's not a good feeling. You feel violated, exposed, unprotected, and vulnerable.

Isaiah said that the Israelites were "snared in holes, and they are hidden in prison houses" (v. 22). That's another terrible condition—to be in a hole and in a prison. It's the feeling of being held captive and bound, not free to do anything.

Verse 22 also says, "They are for a prey." The word *prey* refers to being hunted, chased, or pursued. The Bible describes Satan as a roaring lion seeking whom he may devour (1 Pet. 5:8).

And this is probably the worst part of this passage of Scripture: "And no one delivers" (v. 22). There was no deliverance in sight for the people of Israel. It seemed there was no one who could do anything about their being in that situation. There was no one who would speak the word *restore*. But we know that there was One coming who would bring restoration to Israel, who would break them out of their prison, and who would bring them into a place of fruitfulness and abundance.

Israel's Redemptive History Is the Key to Your Deliverance

As we expose and dismantle the spirit of rejection, you will notice that I will frequently refer back to God's covenant nation, the people of Israel; I do so because they are the physical type or foreshadower for what God wants to do in each of our lives spiritually. The people of Israel were double-minded and rebellious. They were rejected and separated from God because of their disobedience and failure to keep His covenant. But still the children of Israel were God's covenant people. Remember the promise God made to Abraham? In Genesis 12:3 God promised Abraham that all families of the earth would be blessed through him. Through Abraham came the promised son, Isaac, and then Jacob (who was renamed Israel) and his twelve sons (the twelve tribes of Israel). From there the genealogy continued to Jesus Christ. This was how God established Israel as His covenant people.

Israel continued to violate their covenant with God. Deuteronomy 28 lists certain stipulations that, if Israel obeyed and kept the covenant, would cause the people to be blessed; however, if the Israelites broke the covenant, they would be cursed. One of the curses that would come upon them would be actual physical captivity and bondage, which would result in the destruction and desolation of their homes, cities, health, and all-around livelihood. Many times God sent prophets such as Isaiah, Jeremiah, and Ezekiel to warn Israel of their covenant violations and to call them to repentance and back to the covenant. If they did not repent, they would face the wrath or judgments of the broken covenant. But if they repented, they would have the mercy of the covenant and God would forgive them and restore them.

Israel did not listen to the prophets. Instead they persecuted them and killed them, and as a result God's covenant judgment and wrath came upon Israel. Then we get to the prophet Jeremiah, who prophesied during the last days of the kings of Israel when judgment was certain. The last godly king that Israel had was Josiah. (See 2 Kings 22–23.) In the eighteenth year of Josiah's reign the book of the covenant, which had been lost because of idolatry, was discovered in the temple. King Josiah began to repent and call Israel back to its covenant with God. However, by the time he did, it was too late. Judgment was already prophesied over Israel. But God told Josiah that since he turned to Him, He would not bring His judgment in his day; He would withhold judgment until after he was gone (2 Kings 22:18–20).

After Josiah's death the kings of Israel went right back into rebellion, disobedience, and apostasy. The last king of Israel was King Zedekiah. He resisted the words of the prophet Jeremiah, who warned him that the king of Babylon, Nebuchadnezzar, was coming. Jeremiah told the king to submit to Nebuchadnezzar because there was no avoiding the seventy years of captivity coming. After seventy years, however, Israel would be restored back to the land.

From reading the books of 2 Kings, 2 Chronicles, and Jeremiah, we know that Nebuchadnezzar did come. He broke down the city, burned it with fire, destroyed many of the Jews, and took the remaining Jews into Babylon. For seventy years the Israelites were captives in Babylon.

The Book of Lamentations, written by the Prophet Jeremiah, describes the desolation of Israel, the judgment that came upon the nation, Jerusalem being burned, and the people being taken into captivity and becoming slaves in Babylon. It describes the mourning, sadness, depression, oppression, and total devastation of this nation. And as you read the Prophets, you need to understand—and this is important for prophetic people—the prophets did not only prophesy judgment; they also prophesied restoration. You see this primarily in Isaiah. After Isaiah prophesies judgment, he says in Isaiah 54:1, "Sing, O barren, you who did not bear a child. Break forth into singing." In Isaiah 60:1 he exhorts, "Arise, shine, for your light has come, and the glory of the LORD has risen upon you." In other words, God is saying through the prophet Isaiah, "Israel, even though you have violated My covenant and My judgment has come upon you, I will still use you and restore you to bless the whole world." This blessing would come through the seed of Abraham—the Messiah, Jesus Christ.

The Bible is not a history book of the entire world. It is only a history of redemption, primarily dealing with one covenant nation. It does not deal with the whole world. There are many nations outside of Israel that are not recorded in the Bible. So as I said, it is only redemptive history. The reason why it is so important to understand this principle is because when you understand redemptive history, you understand redemption, salvation, reconciliation, deliverance, and restoration. You will understand what your salvation is about and what God did to secure it for you. The Bible also shows us the wisdom of God in using a nation that had broken covenant, a nation so full of rebellion and disobedience, to show us the way to covenant with God.

In the Book of Acts, after the coming of the Holy Spirit, we see that salvation began in Jerusalem. The entire church was

Jewish. God used this group, or remnant, to evangelize and bring salvation to the rest of the known world. Paul talks about the remnant in Romans 9 and 11. They are also called the elect. There was always a remnant within Israel—a small group that never forsook God. They always kept covenant. Like in Elijah's day with the seven thousand who remained righteous, there is always that group who will not bow the knee to Baal or kiss his feet. So from the remnant the light of God was shown, and all the nations came into salvation. And here we are—saved because of what God did more than two thousand years ago.

Understanding Israel's progression of going from desolation to restoration should show you this: no matter how much your life has been devastated, no matter how much desolation, ruin, pain, hurt, and rejection has come into your life, God is able to restore you. That's good news. His mercy, grace, and kindness can come into your life, and that's what deliverance is all about. Deliverance is about being restored.

By His Stripes We Are Healed

Isaiah 53:5 says, "He was wounded for our transgressions, he was bruised for our iniquities; the chastisement of our peace was upon him, and by his stripes we are healed." That word *healed* is not only talking about physical healing. It also refers to restoration. Israel would receive healing and restoration through the suffering and travail of Jesus, the Messiah.

As Christ suffered and died on the cross, He did not die just for you to go to heaven and not go to hell. He died so you could be healed and restored. He died so you could have life and have it more abundantly while you are here on this earth. God does not want you broken up, messed up, confused, depressed, and sad. He does not want your life to be a living hell while you are here, but one day in the by-and-by you're going to heaven. He wants you to have life and have it more abundantly; He wants to heal you and restore you.

The Lord is releasing this word to you today: "I am here to restore you and to return to you the years the locust have eaten. You will no longer be rejected. You will not be left in ruin. You will come to Me, and I will accept you." Though it may seem that there is no one who will deliver a word of restoration into your life, the Lord is sending a word today to say, "Be restored!"

In this book we are going to expose the destructive spirit of rejection so that you will learn how to be set free, how to restore the broken places in your life, and how to walk in the blessing and abundance of God.

Rejection is not for you. God wants you to be free to love and to be loved. It is His whole plan for your life to know you can be fully accepted by Him through His Son. The spirit of rejection keeps you from being able to see and accept the perfect love that God has for you. Rejection needs to be broken from your life. The first step in doing that is identifying its roots in your life and then applying spiritual strategies to cast it out so that you can be the stable person God wants you to be.

[PART I]

THE DESOLATION OF REJECTION

CHAPTER 1

HOW DOES REJECTION ENTER?

Having prayed for believers of many nations, I have come to this conclusion: the greatest undiagnosed, therefore, untreated malady in the body of Christ today is rejection. Rejection, whether active or passive, real or imaginary, robs Jesus Christ of His rightful lordship in the life of His children and robs them of the vitality and quality of life that Jesus intended.[1]

—NOEL AND PHYL GIBSON

AN OPEN DOOR to rejection comes when we do not receive the love and acceptance God created us to receive. Being loved and accepted is one of our basic human needs. We sometimes try to be strong and say we don't need anyone or that we don't care what people think. But this is not completely true; this may actually be a sign that we have experienced rejection at some point. God created in us a desire to love and to be loved and accepted. We need love from our families and from others. We especially need the love of God.

If we don't get that love, we feel and experience rejection, which often manifests itself as either fear or pride. These are the two strongest manifestations of rejection. Fear says, "I can no longer trust anyone. I have been hurt too badly, so I am afraid of commitment and close relationships." Pride says, "I can do better by myself. Everyone has hurt me, and because of that I don't need anyone in my life. I don't need help. I can make my own way." The enemy knows how to destroy us through rejection, and he will use fear and pride to open the door for all kinds of demonic oppression to come into our lives.

Rejection is one of the most common demons we deal with in deliverance ministry. It is the basis for double-mindedness. Rejection opens the door for rebellion, which gives the enemy a chance to set up two demonic personalities within an individual and suppress his or her personality so that a stable identity is never fully developed. The person grows up double-minded with rejection as the inward personality and rebellion as the outward personality.

Frank and Ida Mae Hammond are pioneers in discovering the link between rejection and rebellion as they relate to double-mindedness. They wrote the classic deliverance book *Pigs in the Parlor*, where this revelation of double-mindedness and schizophrenia is defined and explored. While ministering with Frank and Ida Mae before they passed, I found them both to be humble and gracious. When they laid hands on me and imparted their mantle to teach and minister on this subject, I was filled with a passion to see people set free from this spirit. It is something that drives the core of my deliverance ministry even to this day.

As I have learned from studying their teachings, my own Bible study, and experience in ministry, two main strongholds make up the double-minded personality: rejection and rebellion, with the root of bitterness coming in secondarily. They interact like a threefold cord and are not easily broken.

Rejection is the doorway to double-mindedness. Demons associated with rejection make it almost impossible for individuals to develop into the true people God created them to be. They become ruled by these spirits and find themselves always trying to compensate for their lack of development and lack of confidence. They become rebellious in order to protect themselves from hurt and being taken advantage of. With rebellion comes bitterness—bitterness against people and life circumstances that have caused all kinds of hurt and trauma.

Many people don't realize they have been rejected and how they themselves continue the cycle of rejection in their lives. You have mostly likely experienced the ripple effect of rejection throughout your life from parents, relatives, teachers, church leaders, supervisors, coworkers, and spouses who have been hurt and rejected and have reacted to you out of that spirit, causing you to experience rejection.

While everyone has been rejected, not everyone will become schizophrenic or what is referred to as double-minded in James 1:8: "A double-minded man is unstable in all his ways." It's all about whether or not you are able to develop a stable personality. So you can be rejected and not be schizophrenic. But everyone who is schizophrenic or double-minded has been rejected.

To give some background, the term *schizophrenia* sometimes means split personality or split mind. *Schizo* is a Greek word that means "to rend, tear violently, open or unfold."[2] Severe schizophrenia is treated by psychiatry with drugs and, as history shows, even with shock treatment due to hallucinations and delusion (mental illness and insanity). Schizophrenia can occur in various degrees, with most not requiring a person to be hospitalized.

In the early nineteenth century psychologists identified dissociative identity disorder and adopted the term "alter ego" (from the Latin for "the other I"), which is often defined as the second self, a second personality or persona within a person. Often the core personality is not aware of the actions performed by the alternate persona. People who have alter egos lead double lives. They operate through extreme dysfunction with multiple distinct personalities called "alters." I see them as demons. Demons have distinct personalities and can enter a person's life causing them to act in uncharacteristic ways, such as in the story of the demonized man in Mark 5.

Rejection From the Womb

Rejection often begins at a young age; it can even start in the womb through prenatal curses, being unwanted or illegitimate, abandonment, birth order, adoption, or molestation. A person may receive a spirit of rejection because of the manner or timing of conception; for example, if the mother was raped or molested or was having an extramarital affair and became pregnant. Children born under these circumstances may show a spirit of rejection. Also, children born out of wedlock or to parents who did not want them or who are a strain on the family budget, the last of a large family, or the middle child of a family often struggle with rejection.

Another form of prenatal rejection is when the parents desperately want to have a child of a specific gender but find out that the child they are having will be of the opposite gender. All their prayers and hopes are focused toward having a child of a certain gender. But when the child is born of the opposite gender, that child is rejected or abandoned. This is common in certain cultures where one gender is given privilege and status over the other.

The birthing experience can affect how a child feels either loved and received or abandoned and rejected. If a child was forced out of the birth canal with forceps or a vacuum, for instance, he or she may have difficulty adjusting to life outside of the womb. The natural birthing process allows hormones and other psychological transitions to take place that naturally prepare a baby to adjust to the new environment. Sudden exposure to noise, bright lights, and physical handling after the warmth and security of the womb can be traumatic. Being born after long and protracted labor in which the mother and the baby have both become exhausted or being born by C-section may also cause some children to develop a spirit of rejection.

Mother and baby bonding after birth is another place in early life where a child is assured of his or her place in the family and in life. If this bonding does not happen due to health issues on the part of the baby or the mother or for other reasons, the baby may sense rejection. This may also be why some adopted children suffer from a spirit of rejection.

Generational Rejection

Rejection can be passed down through the generations of a family. Parents who have suffered from hereditary rejection, or who have been rejected before marriage, find it hard to show love and affection to their children. Of course they love their children, but because they don't come from a family that showed physical affection or said, "I love you," "I'm proud of you," or other expressions of worth and value, they are unable to express love through physical contact. It is not uncommon to hear a parent say, "We are not an affectionate family," or "We don't kiss and hug all over each other." This is sometimes read as, "There is something shameful about physical affection. Therefore we are embarrassed to express it in that way."

Though material things such as gifts, clothes, a nice bedroom, and toys are used to show love, some children still grow up feeling rejected and insecure. Others grow up in homes where there is poverty and a feeling of never having enough. Children who grow up in homes like this can also feel rejected if the parents are ashamed or fear that they are not able to adequately provide for their family.

In your own experiences you may have heard of instances where a father wanted a son but instead had a girl, yet he still treated her as if she were his son by pushing her to participate in certain activities, wear certain clothes, or behave in boyish ways. The same thing can happen with mothers who want a girl but ended up giving birth to a boy. Other deliverance ministers have pointed out that this could be the root of the gender issues many gay, lesbian, bisexual, and transgender individuals deal with.

A person can also be rejected by their family. This kind of rejection can be the result of abandonment by one or both parents (whether intentional or perceived), abuse from authority figures (either emotional or physical), being put into foster care, being put up for adoption, being born with birth defects, experiencing the death of parent, parental neglect, or having overbearing or perfectionist parents. And as I mentioned earlier, birth order can sometimes be the root. Middle children can be vulnerable if they feel the parents favor the elder or younger siblings.

More Ways Rejection Enters During Early Stages of Life

Other kinds of rejection can come from being teased, bullied, stereotyped, or held back or restricted from certain activities in school because of how an individual looks, one's race, social and economic differences, gender, disability, or body type. Here are more ways rejection can enter in early life:

From parents' relationship to each other

- Witnessing the father abuse the mother—sexually, verbally, or physically
- Living in a home with unhappy parents who argue, fight, or won't talk to each other, only speaking to their children, which causes the children to feel guilty and responsible
- Living in a home where one or both parents are alcoholics or drug abusers

From parents' relationship to their children

- Being parented by a weak, apathetic, or passive father
- Being constantly criticized and made to feel like one can never measure up
- Being raised by parents who show no active interest in one's progress in school, sports activities, or leisure time
- Being raised by parents who have abundant financial resources but are stingy and withhold provision from their children
- Being parented by a father who shows more attention to his daughter's girlfriends than he does to his own daughter
- Being consistently left home alone because of the parents' working hours or their disinterest in their children's welfare

- Experiencing parental harshness or coldness
- Never receiving forgiveness or a sense of being trusted by one's parents
- Being used to getting one's own way and regularly receiving preferential treatment—being spoiled
- Being bribed or threatened to be academically successful

From sibling dynamics

- Having a terminally ill or mentally challenged sibling who requires extensive medical care and attention
- Receiving discipline that seems unfair, especially when it seems as if another member of the family always gets a pass and is everyone's favorite

From life-changing events or trauma

- Living through a fire or natural disaster by which the family home was destroyed
- Having a close relative who committed a serious crime and is sentenced to serve prison time
- Being a victim of sexual abuse or incest
- Experiencing a sudden decline in family's socio-economic status due to unemployment, under-employment, or bankruptcy

From involuntary physical characteristics

- Being part of a racial minority

- Suffering from a speech impediment such as stuttering, stammering, lisping, or an inability to pronounce certain consonants or words
- Being teased, bullied, or called names because of uncommon physical features

From school, church, and other social groups

- Being expelled from school for bad behavior
- Being excluded from a desired social group; i.e., "the cool kids"
- Being embarrassed by parents' religious beliefs

A Special Word on Parental Rejection

Parental rejection is a very big open door to the enemy. All of us need love and approval, and we should get that approval from our parents. You can probably recall times when you were let down by your parents in significant ways, which left you open to rejection. If you are struggling with issues of rejection and are reading this book for your own deliverance, know that you are preparing yourself to be the parent your children will need and perhaps the parent you didn't have. It is your job to be watchful so that the enemy will not use you to plant seeds of bitterness and rejection in the hearts of your children. The enemy will try to repeat the same patterns of rejection you experienced and keep these patterns going from generation to generation.

The devil tries to work on children at a young age, and through their parents he will try to plant a seed of rejection in their hearts, causing them to grow up bitter and angry. This is why children need to go through deliverance.

Looking around America today, we can see that there are a lot of angry young people. They are angry with their parents because their parents have not loved them, spent time with them, or raised them up in the things of God. Many young people have been born out of wedlock. Their fathers are not in the home, so they have no fatherly image. Mother and father are separated, divorced, or were never married. So when we see young people involved in all kinds of ungodly and perverse activities, we can't just blame the devil for it. The devil couldn't get in unless a parent opened the door by not providing a prayer covering, love, and security.

The devil's plan is to break down marriages and bring in unfaithfulness, separation, and divorce. He knows what that kind of breakdown does to the generations that follow. He knows how a child will feel in a custody battle or when the mother has to go to court to collect child support and the father won't willingly pay to support his children. He knows how a seed of rejection has the potential to grow until the person's life is left in ruin.

Of course all situations aren't like this. All men are not looking to shed the responsibility of a family. I don't want to stir up any man-hating spirits. There are some great fathers out there who love their children, and there are strong men and women who are thriving in godly relationships and raising great children. But consider the consequences when this is not the case, which oftentimes it is not. Yes, mom is there, and she may be a powerful and godly woman who is able to teach, preach, prophesy, and cast out devils. But there is no substitute for a committed father in the home. There is an order God has established for the home that provides a defense against the enemy's attacks on our young people.

You must remember that the devil is not just after you; he's after your seed. We cannot afford to be selfish in this area, only thinking about what benefits us. It is your responsibility as a parent to raise your children according to the Word of God.

So, yes, the blame for what is happening with our young people mainly rests on the parents. We cannot, in America, have high divorce rates, shack up and sleep with multiple partners, and do whatever we want to do and expect our children to be OK. We have a messed-up generation. Homosexuality, lesbianism, bisexuality, and gender confusion are running rampant among our youth. This is a spirit of perversion with roots that began in rejection.

Because they have been rejected, these youth are angry and upset; what we tell them not to do, they are anxiously running to do. Half of the time we don't know what our young people are doing when they leave the house. Some seem to have no interest in church or God—and we're left wondering what happened. Well, as we have discussed, it started early on in their young lives.

However, we can have the confidence that God has a plan to restore all the years the locusts have eaten. You may not have made the right choices about whom you hooked up with or what stage of life you were in when you brought a new life into the world. But as you grow in the knowledge of God, you can repent and get delivered and restored, so that your children and your children's children will be shielded from the enemy. You can begin to repair the breaches, so that they can walk in the covenant blessings of the Lord all the days of their lives.

The cycle of rejection, bitterness, and anger can stop with you. Once you've been set free, your past choices do not have to ruin your life. You can confidently say, "I am going to walk with God.

God is going to forgive me and bless me. I am going to raise my child the best way I can. I am going to bind the devil. I am going to protect my child and bring him or her up in the fear of God. I'm going to get around the anointing and the glory of God. My child and I are going to get under a good spiritual covering, a good church, and we are going to submit to spiritual authority. The devil cannot have my child. Devil, you are a liar."

Single parents, do this: if you are not already connected with a good church, find one with a godly pastor, and get under his godly covering and authority. If you are a single mom, or even a single father needing help and support, you don't have to be out in the world trying to fight off devils and trying to get through society without any godly support. But specifically for single moms, God made women to be covered. (See 1 Corinthians 11:3.) This is not about superiority, for "there is neither Jew nor Greek, there is neither slave nor free, and there is neither male nor female, for you are all one in Christ Jesus" (Gal. 3:28). We are all part of the seed of Abraham. We've been freed from any curse that subjugates women. What I am talking about here is divine order. So if your father is not a believer or is not providing spiritual covering for you as a single woman, find a trustworthy apostolic father. Children and women were made to be covered. You weren't made to be out in the world alone and unprotected.

Abuse and Trauma Can Open the Door to Rejection

Another way that we can become tormented by rejection is through abuse or trauma. Physical, sexual, and verbal abuse are some of the most damaging things a person can go through. These experiences can leave scars on a person's emotions to the point that some fail to develop and mature past the point in their lives that the abuse occurred. They become stuck and unable to move past that season of their life. Abuse opens the door to various manifestations of rejection, such as self-rejection and self-hate, where the person either takes on self-destructive behaviors, such as cutting and eating disorders, or develops a spirit of infirmity, as we'll see in a later chapter. An individual can also develop a broken heart, finding it difficult to sustain healthy relationships with others and impossible to move past the memory of the events. Without strong prayer and deliverance, many can find themselves to be what has been called unlucky in love.

Demons can enter our lives through traumatic experiences. *Webster's* defines *trauma* as "a disordered psychic or behavioral state resulting from severe mental or emotional stress or physical injury."[3]

Rape and incest are among the most prevalent and devastating experiences people around the world and throughout history have lived through. Let's look at them now and see how they open the door to rejection.

Sexual violation by rape

Over the course of a lifetime a person can experience many difficulties, but some of the most life-altering challenges involve sexual violations against one's physical body. Sexual assault or abuse is a violation that results in not only physical injury but also deep emotional scars. This ungodly act can be an open door for oppression by the enemy, often leaving a wake of destruction, depression, and manifestations of low self-worth to wreak havoc on the victim's life.

As a result of being raped or sexually abused, a person may exhibit hurt, distrust, lust, perversion, anger, hatred, rage, bitterness, shame, guilt, and fear. These are all manifestations of the rejection side of the double-minded spirit. If not discerned and cast out, demons take advantage of individuals in their weakened state, setting traps and vices to torment them for the rest of their lives. Sexual violations such as rape can also be part of a generational curse. During deliverance ministry it is sometimes discovered that a history of rape and sexual abuse has recurred throughout the bloodline.

If you were to closely examine the history of an oppressed people—consider blacks in America, Jews during Hitler's regime, and some of the ethnic cleansings in Africa and other parts of the world—rape has always been part of dominating and controlling a people. In Lamentations 5 there is evidence of this very thing in the history of the people of Israel. Verse 11 says, "They have raped the women in Zion, the virgins in the towns of Judah" (JB).

Being raped as part of an oppressed people is shameful and humiliating. Victors in wars have raped (and still rape) the women of conquered people. It is a common, evil practice during such conflicts.

People who have suffered sexual violation and abuse have problems with experiencing sexual intimacy in marriage. They often are so guarded and afraid of being taken advantage of again that they hold back from expressing emotions of love, affection, and desire with their spouses. Some have trouble with hating all men, and they develop deep roots of bitterness. Coping mechanism like these are poisonous to the person's mind, body, and spirit. They often end up with spirits of sickness and infirmity, including some autoimmune diseases and cancer.

Sexual violation through incest

Incest is a violation usually perpetrated by a trusted and well-admired family member. It often leaves victims feeling betrayed, shamed, and guilty for seemingly having brought the act upon themselves. They may ask themselves, "What did I do to make the person think I wanted this?" Incest can also be part of a generational curse.

Victims of incest often feel as if they may go insane with all the torment and guilt brought on by this violation. They may suffer depression and confusion, which may lead to suicidal thoughts and tendencies. With their spiritual door opened wide to seducing spirits, they often are led into sexually perverted, promiscuous, and lustful lifestyles.

Rejection Later in Life

As we grow older, we continue to experience rejection in various ways. The truth of it is that we are always encountering people who have also been rejected, and because of their rejection they reject others—including you. Divorce, the death of a loved one, and even health issues can continue the cycle of rejection into adulthood. Here is a brief list of how rejection shows up later in life:

- Being abandoned or divorced by a spouse
- Being widowed or cheated on by a spouse
- Being physically or mentally mistreated by a spouse
- Feeling shame as a result of being convicted of a criminal offense
- Serving time in prison
- Suffering long-term mental, emotional, or physical issues, and after exhausting all forms of professional help, still remaining ill

- Experiencing difficulty in coming to agreement with a spouse regarding religious beliefs and practices
- Experiencing instability in household finances and maintenance of basic living needs because of a spouse's drug or alcohol addiction
- Experiencing a breakup and heartbreak in a committed romantic relationship
- Living with a permanent disability as a result of disease or an accident
- Being forced to live in challenging circumstances that are out of your control
- Being terminated from a place of employment for incompetency or inability to find employment over a long period of time
- Being betrayed by trusted friends, mentors, or advisors
- Living through financial loss due to making bad investments as a result of advice from a close friend, or being financially cheated by dishonest advisors

Societal, Cultural, or Ethnic Rejection

Racism, prejudice, bigotry, and other forms of oppression due to a person's cultural background, race, or ethnicity leave room for the spirit of rejection to take root. Because one is born into a race or culture, this type of rejection is part of a person's bloodline and is usually impossible to avoid. The person does not have to do anything wrong to be rejected by people; it is simply the color of his skin that causes the rejection. Bitterness, anger, distrust, hate, and retaliation against those by whom the person is rejected often are demonic manifestations of this type of rejection. Victims often experience a higher level of stress, anxiety, and depression as a result of living under seemingly unrelenting limitations and restrictions. The act of being racist is demonic in itself, fueling a demonic response from its victims.

Jesus wants to deliver us all from feeling the need to promote this kind of rejection, and He has set a path of deliverance for us to be set free from being oppressed by it. Though racism and various kinds of prejudice are not often discussed in our churches, they were brought to light and confronted in the Bible. Let's take a look at a couple examples.

The story of Esau contains many different applications when it comes to the spirit of rejection. He was rejected because he sold his birthright, but this initial rejection led to a progression through which all of his descendants became open to rejection because of their bloodline.

> ...lest there be any sexually immoral or profane person, as Esau, who for one morsel of food sold his birthright. For you know that afterward, when he wanted to inherit the blessing, *he was rejected*. For he found no place for repentance, though he sought it diligently with tears.
>
> —Hebrews 12:16–17, emphasis added

The descendants of Abraham's son Ishmael, known today as Arabic people, carry a strong spirit of rejection. We hear of recurring conflicts in their part of the world that have dated back to ancient history. Jewish people have suffered rejection throughout history as well—from Bible times, to the Crusades, and on to the Holocaust.

Making it clear that discrimination of this type is not pleasing to His Father, Jesus deliberately traveled through Samaria although traditionally Jews and Samaritans hated each other. His purpose in exposing the bigoted hearts of the people in His day was a message of equality for us today. (See John 4.) Even in the early church, prejudice and racism between Jews and Gentiles were major behaviors the apostles condemned.

When people who have suffered racial, ethnic, or cultural rejection come to Christ, they will need deliverance. Many African Americans need deliverance in this area because of generational issues dating back to American slavery. Native Americans are another group who have been severely oppressed generation after generation. They too will need major deliverance as they accept Christ.

God does not play favorites with any one group of people over another. Black, Native American, Jewish, Samaritan, Arabic, and any other people who have suffered rejection because of who they are can find deliverance and healing in Him. The history of certain people does not dictate their future. In Christ you can be set free even if societal norms of rejection don't seem to change. Pride, fear, anger, depression, low self-esteem, victim mentality, inferiority, poverty, and all the other demons that manifest as a result of this kind of rejection do not have to be your lot.

Next we are going to look at rejection from another perspective—divine rejection. We don't teach this aspect of rejection very much in the church because we want people to know that God is love. While it is true that God is love, He still has standards and will not accept everything. Depending on the way divine rejection is handled, it can also bring ruin to our lives if we are not careful.

CHAPTER 2

REJECTED BY GOD?

My people are destroyed for lack of knowledge. Because you have rejected knowledge, I will reject you.

—HOSEA 4:6

SO FAR WE'VE discussed rejection that occurs when someone has been rejected by another person such as a parent or they've grown up in a bad situation. We've looked at how sexual abuse can lead to a spirit of rejection, causing a person to have difficulties with relationships. We've also discussed self-rejection, fear of rejection, guilt, shame, pride, and many other demonic spirits that enter as a result of rejection. Ultimately these spirits form a basis for double-mindedness and instability. In this chapter I am going to deal with rejection from a different angle than what is usually taught. I want to take a look at divine rejection—the fact that God rejects people and lifestyles.

The reason I want to deal with this is because we've begun to believe that God never rejects anyone, that God is love, and that He forgives us no matter what we have done—and this is true. But we sometimes forget that God is also holy and His standard is holiness. As people of God we should want to remain in a place in which we are pleasing to God and growing in His knowledge. We don't want to get on a path of disobedience and rebellion, like the people of Israel, which will ultimately lead to destruction and desolation. Therefore we need to understand that God does have a standard, and as His covenant people we should be moving in the direction of being holy as He is holy. Everything that happens in life is not holy and acceptable to God.

Even in the light of this revelation, I must also point out Jesus's words in John 6:37: "The one who comes to Me I will by no means cast out" (NKJV). So we can be confident that He will never reject anyone who repents and comes to God in faith. Jesus tells us, "Come to Me, all you who labor and are heavily burdened, and I will give you rest" (Matt. 11:28). God encourages people. He is no respecter of persons. He doesn't reject people based on their color, culture, or gender. God is love and will never reject anyone who comes to Him in faith, love, and repentance. But there are some behaviors and lifestyles that God cannot receive or accept. If we choose to remain in them, God will release us out of His care and into the lifestyle we've chosen. So in essence, as I will point out, we are first rejecting God.

Biblical References to Divine Rejection

When we teach that God accepts all people no matter what, we are not accurately reflecting His standards as they are set out in His Word. The Bible records many stories that reveal God's rejection of certain behaviors and lifestyles. In Genesis 3 we see that Adam, the first man God created, was rejected by God for disobeying His command to not eat of the tree of the knowledge of good and evil. Adam ate of the tree and was cast out of the Garden of Eden as a result.

Next up was Cain, who offered a sacrifice the Lord rejected. Instead of correcting his mistake, Cain became jealous of his brother, Abel, because God accepted Abel's sacrifice. Fully manifesting a spirit of rejection, Cain allowed anger and bitterness to drive him to kill Abel (Gen. 4:3–10).

Because Abraham and Sarah did not want to wait for God's promise to be fulfilled, they took matters into their own hands. Their actions led to a whole people group being rejected generation after generation. We talked about the Ishmaelites' societal rejection briefly in the last chapter.

Ishmael, conceived out of an unwillingness to wait on God, was also rejected by God (Gen. 21:8–21). Abraham and Sarah had tried to help God by using Sarah's maid, Hagar, as a surrogate. (See Genesis 16:1–4.) But this was not God's plan, and He did not need their help. Therefore Ishmael was rejected as the promised son. Understand that it wasn't that God didn't love Ishmael, because He did, just as He loves us all. It was simply the fact that Ishmael was not the one whom God promised to Abraham.

First Samuel 15:17 provides an example of another person who experienced divine rejection: "When you were little in your own sight, were you not made the head of the tribes of Israel?" In this verse the prophet Samuel is reminding Saul of who he was before he became king of Israel. Coming from the tribe of Benjamin—the smallest of Israel's tribes—Saul entered the scene predisposed to the spirits of self-rejection, inferiority, and insecurity. Initially God chose and anointed him to be the first king of Israel. But throughout Saul's rule the spirit of rejection and other strongholds began to manifest more and more. He became rebellious and disobedient, choosing to seek his own way ahead of God's. He refused to submit himself to the leading and guiding of the Holy Spirit through the prophet Samuel. This arrogance and pride led him to be rejected by God as king of Israel.

> Behold, to obey is better than sacrifice, and to heed than the fat of rams. For rebellion is as the sin of witchcraft, and stubbornness is as iniquity and idolatry. *Because you have rejected the word of the Lord, He also has rejected you from being king.*
>
> —1 Samuel 15:22–23, nkjv, emphasis added

Though divine rejection opened up Saul's life to demons of paranoia, suspicion, a murderous spirit, witchcraft, and suicide, we must understand that it was Saul who first rejected God. Of course, God's intention was not to get back at Saul, but there were certain commands and instructions through which God wanted to bless and prosper Saul and the people of Israel. Saul's determination to go against what God directed him to do set him on a path of destruction. He forfeited the blessing, protection, and victory over the enemy that obedience and submission to God bring. The story of Saul's rejection demonstrates how demons of rejection can completely ruin a person's whole life.

Rejecting the Knowledge of God Opens the Door to Destruction

Being rejected by God comes as a result of a person's refusal of the knowledge of God.

> My people are destroyed for lack of knowledge. Because you have rejected knowledge, I will reject you from being My priest. And because you have forgotten the law of your God, I will also forget your children.
>
> —Hosea 4:6

This verse defines the curse of rejection, also known as the demon of rejection. This curse or demonic spirit is not just about being turned down or rejected by someone one day. The demon of rejection that enters as a result of refusing the knowledge of God is about your whole life being characterized by the manifestations of this demon, which we will explore in later chapters. Though all of us have been rejected in one way or another, there is a deeper infiltration of the spirit, curse, or demon of rejection that destroys lives and causes one to reject God. But there is deliverance, and there is forgiveness.

God is always open to a person with a repentant and humble heart. If you come to Him in the midst of your mess and confess that you want to know His ways, that you want to walk in the knowledge, wisdom, and understanding of His Word, He will deliver you from the destruction of rejection.

However, God cannot accept you when you are living in deliberate opposition to His ways. He will reject you if you reject deliverance, His Word, and the leading of His Spirit. We are living in a time when hardly any of us can say we have not been introduced to the knowledge of God. There may be remote groups of people who have never known the God of the Bible, but most of us have, in one way or another, been presented with an opportunity to receive the truth of God, deliverance, and healing. So if we choose to go another way and our minds are fixed on living out that choice, God says, "I will reject you."

Hosea 4:6 says it clearly: "Because you have rejected knowledge, I will reject you." So it is not only about a lack of exposure to the knowledge of God; it is also about refusal to accept it. And through our rejection of this knowledge, we are destroyed. Now focus in on that word *destroyed* in this verse.

The spirit of destruction comes into our lives as a result of our rejection of God and then by His rejection of us. If we want to experience victory, blessing, and protection from God—and even acceptance, because we always have His love—it is important for us to repent and accept His truth. We need to be humbly open and submitted to the work of the Holy Spirit in our lives.

Rejecting God Leads to a Reprobate Mind

> And even as they did not like to retain God in their knowledge, God gave them over to a reprobate mind, to do those things which are not convenient [proper (MEV)].
>
> —Romans 1:28, KJV

Continual rejection of God and His ways will cause your mind to be given over to a place of evil and confused rationalization that will lead you to destruction. This is what we saw with Saul. As we come into an understanding of Romans 1:28, we can discern that as a result of divine rejection, Saul was given over to a reprobate mind. The word *reprobate* means "rejected as worthless; morally corrupt."[1] It speaks of a person whose very mindset, rationalizations, and thinking processes have been rejected by God.

We will find a whole kingdom of demons in Romans 1:29–31 that characterize a reprobate mind: "unrighteousness, sexual immorality, wickedness, covetousness, maliciousness; full of envy, murder, strife, deceit, evil-mindedness; they are whisperers, backbiters, haters of God, violent, proud, boasters, inventors of evil things, disobedient to parents, undiscerning, untrustworthy, unloving, unforgiving, unmerciful" (NKJV).

It may be hard to believe that individuals who once walked with God can come to a place where demons take over and wreak havoc in their lives, causing them utter devastation and destruction. But this is the place any of us could end up when God rejects us and we are given over to a reprobate mind. We may not hear this preached from the pulpit in our churches today, but the Bible provides a picture of divine rejection that cannot be disputed. From Cain to Saul, and even the children of Israel, God reveals that He has a set standard for living that He will accept. The guidelines He has provided do not bring harm. They are meant for our prosperity and blessing. But when we disobey His commandments, we are not blessed and protected, and we cannot experience victory over the enemy. When this hedge of protection—His acceptance—is removed, we are exposed and vulnerable.

Not only is the hedge of protection removed, but also we will experience the same rejection as the children of Israel experienced. They were put out of the Promised Land and led as captives to Babylon. God even rejected the priest Eli because he would not correct his sons. Eli was rejected and the priesthood was taken from him. (See 1 Samuel 2:12–4:18.) God will not allow just anything, any behavior, any kind of regard toward Him to go on without consequences. There are conditions to experiencing His blessing and favor.

To bring it forward to contemporary times, we are facing the issue of gay marriage. This is a behavior that is listed among the abominations that follow man being given over to a reprobate mind. (See Romans 1:26–27.) While the government has proven they can and will do what seems good in their eyes, the fact is that God rejects marriages between two people of the same gender. That was not and is not His design, and what man has tried to redefine and make lawful will never be blessed by God.

Advocacy groups are fighting for the homosexual lifestyle and other perverse lifestyles to become an accepted part of society, so much so that their very mind-sets and rationale are reprobate. They have crossed the line. They have rejected God and His design for families and marriages. They are so swept up in their own knowledge that they don't realize God has rejected them. They continue on, like Saul, thinking they are acting righteously when in fact the Spirit of God is not with them.

There are many believers who have taken up this fight as well, and I would warn you to reconsider your position. Though many preachers and theologians are saying that the Bible is outdated in this area or that what it says has not been interpreted correctly, be assured that God is not mocked. He is not a man that He should lie. His design for marriage is that it remains as a holy covenant between a man and a woman. He created them as male and female to be fruitful and multiply (Gen. 1:28). If you are aligning with those who are promoting anything different, realize that you are choosing to reject the truth of God's Word, and you are in position to be rejected by Him.

This is a real and present danger many are denying in these days and times. But God does not accept just anything. He only accepts that which is worthy of His acceptance. He doesn't accept just any kind of sacrifice, offering, or lifestyle.

You Can't Live Any Way You Want and Be Accepted

Somehow we have taken the fact that God is love to mean that God has no standard for His people. Of course, you can come to Him as you are, but the way that you experience His fullness is by coming to Him humbly and submitted, expecting to exchange your ways for His. We come to God through Jesus and receive the gift of salvation. Then the Holy Spirit begins the work of delivering us and setting us free, transforming us into His likeness.

People think God just accepts everything and everybody. They think they can do anything and God will still accept them. Basically they are believing that He will accept unrighteousness, sexual immorality, wickedness, covetousness, maliciousness, envy, murder, strife, deceit, gossip, slander, violence, anger, pride, boasting, and disobedience. (See Romans 1:29–30.) However, those within the church who believe in an all-accepting God may quickly reject these things and say, "That's not what I mean." But isn't it?

We can be so mushy-gushy with the love of God that we never feel that any behavior should be condemned or dealt with. We've become so tolerant of everything because God is love that we never ever judge. Even I find myself hating to use the word *judge*, but Jesus did say, "Judge with righteous judgment" (John 7:24, NKJV). So there are some things we do have to judge. If there are two individuals in a church who are engaging in sexual sin, that behavior has to be judged by the leaders of the church. As a leader especially, you cannot allow people to live ungodly lifestyles if you know about it. You are responsible for helping them along in their relationship with God and other people. The apostle Paul was quick to deal with ungodly behavior and teaching, not only because of the influence both have on the person, but also because of what they can do to the body of Christ.

> It is actually reported that there is sexual immorality among you, and such immorality as is not even named among the Gentiles, that a man has his father's wife. But you are arrogant. Instead you should have mourned, so that he who has done this deed might be removed from among you.... Your boasting is not good. Do you not know that a little yeast leavens the whole batch? Therefore purge out the old yeast, that you may be a new batch, since you are unleavened.
>
> —1 Corinthians 5:1–7

Here, Paul is talking not only about the sin but also how the church dealt with the sin that was made known to them—the sin that was committed out in the open. The church leaders let it go and did not judge it. They did not seek to correct it, nor did they seek to bring the person to deliverance, counseling, prayer, and restoration. They just let the behaviors that God Himself rejects dwell among them.

Now there are people who are always doing things that we may not know about. They are hiding, though they can't stay hidden for too long. What is done in the dark must come to light (Mark 4:22; Luke 8:17). But there are others openly living in sin who feel as if they can live with ungodly and unrighteous behaviors and no one should say anything to them about it. But that is not what the Bible says. Especially within the body of Christ we should be quick to call attention to immoral behavior and wrong teaching.

> I wrote to you in my letter not to keep company with sexually immoral people. Yet I did not mean the sexually immoral people of this world, or the covetous and extortioners, or the idolaters, since you would then need to go out of the world.... But God judges those who are outside. Therefore "put away from among yourselves that wicked person."
>
> —1 Corinthians 5:9–10, 13

Paul makes it clear that judgment of those who are not in the kingdom is for God, but within the kingdom there is a standard. This is why I believe so strongly in the prophetic anointing. Prophets will have the discernment and anointing to see and call out things happening in the church that are not of God. Prophetic churches are where the standard of the Lord is held high.

Even though there are some people who will actually intimidate you into thinking you cannot say anything corrective to them about their lifestyle choices, if they are honest, they know life does not work that way. When you grow up and learn more about life, you begin to understand that someone will always be there to judge your actions. If you commit a crime, law enforcement will come and arrest you. You will be prosecuted. There is a judge before whom you will stand. And you can't stand before him and say, "Well, the Bible says, 'Judge not.'" You can't live a lifestyle of crime, breaking laws and becoming a danger to society, and not expect for someone to judge you.

The whole purpose for law, order, police, judges, and attorneys is so that we can restrain people who could potentially become threats to society. And we have a right to enjoy peace and prosperity. The US Constitution says that we are all endowed by our Creator with certain inalienable rights, and that we should be able to pursue three things: life, liberty, and happiness. Every one of us should be able to enjoy these rights. That's not the Bible; that's the Constitution. So if there are people running around unrestrained and lawless, their actions will not only destroy their lives but will also put at risk your life, liberty, and happiness.

The American society has established a standard that tries to prevent that from happening. The kingdom of God is a holy, set-apart society with checks and balances in place that prevent us from putting at risk our chances of living in the fullness of the glory and presence of God. Therefore, just as there are certain things we can't do as we live in an earthly society with other people, there are things we cannot do as kingdom citizens. Although the kingdom of God and earthly societies may differ in what is acceptable, our actions will be judged in both places, and some of them will be rejected. Should we fail to adhere to these requirements, we can be cast out of either society if we choose to live in ways that violate the laws.

If we are seeking to live in the kingdom of God and to have the blessing and favor of God on our lives, we must know that He has requirements for how we live. And according to His Word, there are lifestyles He completely rejects.

God Will Always Reject Disobedience

Notice this in 1 Samuel 16:1: "The Lord said to Samuel, 'How long will you mourn for Saul, since I have rejected him from ruling over Israel? Fill your horn with oil and go. I will send you to Jesse the Bethlehemite, for I have chosen a king for Myself from among his sons.'" So Saul was rejected from being the king. He was rejected from the position that God had anointed him to fill because he rejected the instruction of the Lord, became rebellious, and then tried to get God to accept what he decided to do.

> Then he offered the burnt offering. When he finished offering the burnt offering, Samuel came. And Saul went out to meet him to greet him.
>
> Samuel said, "What have you done?"
>
> And Saul said, "Because I saw that the people were scattered from me, and that you did not come to the appointed assembly days, and the Philistines are gathering themselves together at Mikmash, therefore I said, 'The Philistines will come down now upon me to Gilgal, and I have not yet appeased the face of the Lord.' So I forced myself, and offered the burnt offering."
>
> Samuel said to Saul, "You have done foolishly. You have not kept the commandment of the Lord your God, which He commanded you. Truly now, the Lord would have

> established your kingdom over Israel forever. But now your kingdom will not continue."
>
> —1 Samuel 13:9–14

We do this far too frequently today. We try to modify God's standards to match what we want to do. Then we try to present it to Him as if it should be acceptable. This was Cain's sin. But in every circumstance God will reject disobedience, and if we insist on remaining in disobedience, it can result in being rejected by God.

God does not want a sacrifice; He wants obedience. You can bring a sacrifice of praise into the sanctuary and worship harder than everybody else, run around the church, speak in tongues, lay hands on the sick, and even prophesy (Saul prophesied after he had been rejected as king—1 Samuel 19:23–24), and still be rejected by God. Being obedient to God is what shows you receive His Word in your life. Obedience is what shows you love God. Loving God is one of the greatest commandments we can keep. Obedience also shows our faith in God. There are those today who simply do not believe in God or His Word, and they are pushing for lifestyles that prove their disbelief.

As believers we should have no part in any lifestyle that demonstrates a rejection of the knowledge of God and His ways. Of course, when we first receive salvation, we may not know all there is to know about what God wants from His people. But as we grow in the knowledge of God, our behavior should mature and transform. Deliverance ministry allows us to clean out all the trash and rubbish left by the enemy and allows us to build and sustain godly lifestyles.

There will always be new levels in God, and as we discover them, we can repent of our old ways, get delivered from the influence of the enemy in those areas, and begin to walk in obedience. Lust, rejection, hatred, anger, bitterness, and resentment do not have to rule our minds and our spirits. We are no longer slaves to sin. No matter what is going on in the world, we can choose to live lives according to the standard of God and be blessed, favored, and accepted by God. We were all once rejected and separated from God, but because of Jesus that is not the end of the story.

As we move into this next chapter, begin to pray and ask God to show you how the spirit of rejection is controlling your life and what areas in your life need to be closed off to the enemy. We are going to look at how rejection—whether from others, God, or ourselves—sets up a kingdom in our lives. And we are going to develop a strategy to destroy this spirit for good.

CHAPTER 3

DEMONIC MANIFESTATIONS OF REJECTION

He was despised and rejected of men,
a man of sorrows and acquainted with grief.

—ISAIAH 53:3

THE DEMONIC SPIRIT of double-mindedness first enters a person's life through rejection. In the thirty-plus years that I have ministered deliverance to people all over the world, it always surprises me how prevalent this spirit is. Almost every demonized person I have ministered to has a root of rejection that opened the door to all kinds of oppression. As I pointed out previously, the wound of rejection begins early on in a person's life. Many people move through life with hurts and scars that go untreated, and just like a physical injury, they develop an infection—a spiritual infection, so to speak. This infection attracts demons from the north, south, east, and west. These demons feed on the infected wound like parasites. And before long the person is suffering from so many different spiritual maladies that he or she can hardly unravel them to find freedom. This is why deliverance is so important.

Rejection is an identity stealer. Even after it inflicts the initial wound, rejection causes individuals to doubt who they are, to feel as if there is something wrong with them. Then, rejecting themselves, they take on false personalities trying to become a person whom they think people will like. Or they jump to the conclusion that no one will like them, so they begin to move over into rebellion. This is how the spirit of self-rejection, which usually accompanies rejection, manifests itself. The enemy convinces people that the only way to survive is to suppress their real selves and operate in an alternate personality.

Self-rejection, fear of rejection, and the act of rejecting others form the core of the spirit of rejection. Rejection is a hurtful and painful experience that no one likes to go through. Many of us avoid it by almost any means necessary.

The rejection personality is the inward manifestation of double-mindedness, as we'll see in Ahab, one of the kings of Israel. When a person is rejected, he attempts to defend against the hurt by withdrawing or isolating himself. This defense is really fear—fear of being hurt, ridiculed, betrayed, mistreated, or abused all over again. Fear and its manifestations become a stronghold in the life of a person who carries the spirit of rejection.

Rejection is the sense of being unwanted, the agony of desperately wanting people to love you but being convinced they do not. They actually may be loving and accepting, but when you are suffering rejection, you are unable to believe or receive it. There is an aching desire to be a part of something but never feeling that you are. Isaiah wrote about a woman who had suffered a deep and terrible spiritual wound because of rejection.

> For the LORD hath called thee as a woman forsaken and grieved in spirit, and a wife of youth, when thou wast refused, saith thy God.
>
> —ISAIAH 54:6, KJV

To compensate for rejection, some become withdrawn like a turtle in his shell for protection. Others explode with anger and hatred, fighting bitterly against the pain and injustice. Rejected people often spend their lives seeking a meaningful identity outside of a true relationship with God.[1]

Demonic Spirits Associated With Rejection

We have discussed rejection as a personality, but you need to understand that it is also a demon. In the rejection cluster of demons various evil spirits come together, strengthening and deepening the enemy's hold on an individual's life. I have taught about how there are such things as stubborn demons whose roots go deep and that they are harder to cast out than just a regular demon. The demon of rejection is one of these stubborn demons.

Demons behave like gangs. They operate with strategy and prowl upon people who have been made vulnerable because of emotional pain. They are drawn to weakness and especially to people struggling with rejection. There are many demons that make up the demonic kingdom of rejection. They come in and alter the person's intended reality. Instead of operating in the truth of God, a person is bound and controlled by counterfeit spirits. Let's take a look.

Insecurity/inferiority vs. confidence

A person who has been rejected, shot down, disappointed, and denied will often have negative feelings about their worth and value. Many times such individuals lack confidence and suffer from low self-esteem.

Self-accusation vs. forgiveness

Self-accusation leads rejected persons to have great difficulty forgiving themselves and letting themselves off the hook. They overprocess their role in their rejection, often blaming themselves for the hurt they've endured. They believe that something is wrong with them, that they are not good enough, so perhaps all the bad that has happened to them was their fault.

Depression vs. joy

Depression, or what the Bible calls a spirit of heaviness, is the opposite of the joy of the Lord, which strengthens us. A rejected person manifesting a depressed and heavy spirit is also one who is weakened by self-reliance. The enemy will wear down the rejected person, and due to a lack of healthy relationships, such individuals often feel that they are fighting the battles of life alone. They become overwhelmed by life's challenges. We cannot live life isolated, alone, and trusting no one. We will fall into despondency, despair, discouragement, and hopelessness. Some of us get so bogged down in this darkened, hopeless state that we turn to doctors for mood-altering medications. Prescriptions for antidepressants are rising year after year. If left unchecked, depression can drive a person to suicide. Depression can also lead to sleeplessness, alcoholism, and drug abuse.

Perfectionism vs. excellence

Some people who have suffered rejection will try to win approval by attempting to perform every task or assignment perfectly. They are driven by a hope that doing something well enough will put them in position to be accepted and loved. They are doing all they know to do in their bound state to receive the affirmation they need and to avoid being rejected all over again.

This drive for perfection becomes bondage and opens the door to spirits of pride, ego, and vanity. Some of the signs of perfectionist spirits include obsessive-compulsive behavior; rechecking others' work; having legalistic, religious, or Pharisee spirits; and being nitpicky, critical, judgmental, intolerant, frustrated, and hypocritical. Unfortunately people with perfectionist spirits will force others to reject them and drive the rejection they have deeper because they are almost impossible to live with.

Parents who have perfection spirits can be intolerant and overbearing on their children. Perfectionistic spouses are intolerant toward mates. Perfectionistic pastors are intolerant toward members, and so on. Perfectionistic people are intolerant of those who do not meet their standard of perfection.

Perfection can also lead to legalism and religious spirits. The perfectionist hides behind the rule book, and in religious settings this spirit makes the Bible a rule book. This leads to hypocrisy and covering up because perfectionists cannot admit they have broken any rules.

Deliverance is needed for perfectionistic persons so that they can walk in love, compassion, and mercy toward others. Remember, perfectionism is rooted in rejection, and the person seeking deliverance must fall out of agreement with the rejection personality and allow the Lord to develop their real personality.

Pride vs. humility

Pride, which includes both vanity and ego, is a compensation spirit that helps people sustain a look of success and competence though they may be crumbling under the pressures of life. These spirits attempt to make people feel better about themselves. Pride is a strongman, a stubborn demon, in many lives and is not easy to uproot. This demon is personified as

Leviathan in Scripture. We will look more closely at this demon in chapter 6.

Fear vs. faith

Fear includes fear of seemingly small things or issues such as dogs, germs, and the dark. Though some of us may think people should just get over fears like these, they are legitimate and sometimes paralyzing for those suffering from these fears. There are larger, more commonly experienced fears, such as fears of abandonment, failure, hurt, death, authority figures, commitment, confrontation, and not having enough money. There are also extreme fears such as panic, which we will discuss in more depth in the next chapter.

Paranoia vs. trust

I've introduced King Saul already in the chapter on divine rejection. Through his life we see paranoia personified. I will be discussing him again chapter 4 because he also provides us a picture of what it looks like to never receive deliverance from the spirit of rejection. In the Word of God we can see Saul's first deep wound to the point where the demonic presence has matured and fully manifested, completely destroying his life.

Paranoia creates the tendency to be excessively or irrationally suspicious and distrustful of others. There is no objectivity with paranoia. It is fear based on a need to defend one's ego against sometimes imagined scenarios. The person often projects a defense mechanism that often takes the form of megalomania, "an obsession with grandiose or extravagant things or actions."[2] Those who are obsessed with power, fame, and status can often be paranoid, believing everyone is out to take their position from them.

Paranoia can be seen in blaming others, accusation, delusional accusation, and suspicion, and it is rooted in fear. Paranoia is the baseless suspicion of the motives of others. The rejection personality is always questioning the motives of others and judging them without a cause.

Indecision vs. decisiveness

Indecision results in procrastination, compromise, confusion, forgetfulness, and indifference. Indecision is one of the most debilitating problems in life because a forward-moving life is based on decisions. Indifference is an attitude that causes a person to avoid making decisions.

Procrastination is another way of avoiding decisions by just putting it off for a future time. It can also be rooted in the fear of making a decision.

Passivity vs. proactivity

Passivity causes listlessness, lethargy, continual sadness, crying, defeatism, dejection, despair, despondency, discouragement, escapism, fatigue, gloom, gluttony, grief, guilt, heartache, heartbreak, hopelessness, hurt, hyperactivity, indifference, inner hurts, insomnia, laziness, loneliness, mourning, negativity, rejection, self-pity, sorrow, and tiredness. Many times a person fighting passivity will feel as though he is in a "funk," as if he is going nowhere.

I have often taught on the danger of passivity. It immobilizes a person and causes him to withdraw from life. It takes away the natural desire to be assertive and reach to a higher place. Passive people will not pursue and go after what they need to succeed in life. They will let others do it for them.

Lust vs. love

Because rejection can start early in life, many rejected people get involved with sexually immoral relationships at a young age. They are looking for true love but end up in lustful relationships. Lust is a demonic substitute for true love. People who are out of control in this area can form soul ties with others who use and abuse them. The spirit of harlotry can also show up in childhood and teenage years and can be seen in suggestively dressed young women.

Spirits operating within this demon of lust include adultery, fornication, whoredom, harlotry, seduction, sexual impurity, perversion, homosexuality, lesbianism, masturbation, pornography, incest, fantasy, sodomy, and uncleanness.

Lust is not only sexual; it can also manifest as materialism, overindulgence, food addictions (gluttony, bulimia, anorexia, and extreme dieting), drug and alcohol addictions, clothing choices, and so on.

Fantasy vs. reality

Fantasy is all about any mental image, behavior, or belief system that causes the rejected person to escape from reality. The fantasy cluster of demons includes pornography and daydreaming, and it can lead to having excessive hobbies that a person can use to escape reality.

Perversion vs. purity

Though I will provide a closer look at this demonic spirit in chapter 5, let me provide you a brief list of the demons that operate within this evil cluster: homosexuality, lesbianism, fetishes, molestation, and any other sexual activities that do not align with God's design. Perversion, together with self-rejection, will lead people to reject their own sexual identity. Lust and perversion are two of the stronger spirits that operate in the rejection personality.

Unfairness vs. mercy

Fighting for animal, environmental, homosexual, or any other rights becomes the driving force for some rejected people because they are in an all-consuming hunt to acquire fairness—fairness they themselves never received. Because of how they have been treated, they feel that they have gotten the short end of the stick, that life and people are unfair. Though on the surface it seems noble to want to rid the world of unfairness, underneath it all are manifestations of false compassion and false responsibility. Bitterness, anger, rebellion, and resentment are the opposite strongholds of unfairness and rejection, but these are the spirits that turn many of these groups to enacting violence against those who are on the opposing side of their cause. Comparing this to the biblical gift of mercy, we see that true compassion is extended to all who are hurting, not just to those who believe the way we do.

Guilt vs. grace

Psalm 44:15 reads, "My confusion is continually before me, and the shame of my face hath covered me" (KJV). Guilt, which operates in concert with shame and confusion, is a cluster of demons that includes condemnation, unworthiness, and shame. Shame produces a strong sense of guilt, embarrassment, unworthiness, or disgrace.

Sensitivity vs. long-suffering

Easily offended, hurt, and damaged by the words or actions of others, people who are oversensitive because of rejection are hyperaware of how people see them and are afraid to be negative.

Excessive affection for animals vs. a simple appreciation of all of God's creation

People love their pets. They buy them food, play with them, and take them to the vet. But what happens with some of those who have been oppressed by rejection is that they begin to feel affection for their pets that is beyond the norm. We've heard jokes about the crazy cat lady, but this is serious. There is nothing wrong with loving your pets and taking care of them as long as it does not replace or trump meaningful human relationships.

WHAT ARE THE SIGNS AND SYMPTOMS OF A SPIRIT OF REJECTION?

Double-mindedness begins with rejection and opens the door for an unstable identity and personality. Here are some signs and symptoms that a person may have a spirit of rejection:

- A constant desire for physical love and assurance of self-worth
- Addiction
- Attention seeking
- Despair
- Despondency
- Discouragement
- Envy
- Fantasy
- Fears
- Frustration
- Guilt
- Hopelessness
- Impatience
- Inferiority
- Inordinate affection for animals
- Loneliness
- Lust
- Perverseness
- Pride
- Revenge
- Self-rejection
- Sensitivity
- Shame
- Suicide
- Unworthiness
- Vanity
- Withdrawal[3]

Ahab: A Picture of Rejection

We can look at the lives of Ahab and Jezebel and see not only how Ahab personified the spirit of rejection but also how rejection and rebellion function within the double-minded personality. Both Ahab and Jezebel lived lives that consisted of the very things God hates.

Ahab, the seventh king of Israel, "did more evil in the sight of the Lord than all who were before him" (1 Kings 16:30). He promoted and participated in Baal and Ashtoreth worship. He allowed sexual rights—homosexuality, bestiality, and every disgraceful perversion—and prostitution in the temple of God. Men and women volunteered to serve as prostitutes.

Ahab is also known for his double-mindedness. He was often found waffling between righteousness and the ungodly ways of Jezebel, his wife, who was the daughter of a heathen king. She pushed him to incorporate her foreign gods and religious practices into Israel's culture. (See 1 Kings 16:31.) This is one of the reasons God commanded Israel not to take any wives from among the conquered people. They did not have a covenant with God and would not be able to understand how He dealt with them.

Jezebel's influence led Ahab to forget God. First Kings 14:23 states that the people had earlier built up all kinds of images and places of worship to foreign gods in the groves under the trees. Ahab and Jezebel continued with this practice. There is symbolism that I want to point out so that you will see how these acts revealed that he was being controlled not only by a heathen wife but also by the spirit of rejection.

Strong's concordance relates the word *groves,* as it is used in 1 Kings 14:23 (KJV), to Ashtoreth and idolatrous temple worship. These "services" were held outside in the groves of trees near the temple, where huge carvings of both male and female sexual organs were displayed and worshipped.[4]

This is lust and perversion, two demonic spirits that are part of the rejection personality—two spirits that Ahab allowed in because of his relationship to these influences because of his own oppression. Jezebel did her part, but the door was opened through rejection.

The dynamic between Ahab and Jezebel provides for us a picture of how double-mindedness works. Ahab portrays the inward manifestation of double-mindedness (rejection). He was fearful and full of lust, insecurity, and self-pity. He was envious, pouty, and ridden with guilt and shame.

Jezebel is a demonstration of the outward manifestation of double-mindedness (rebellion). She was stubborn, self-willed, selfish, confrontational, controlling, possessive, and full of hatred, resentment, bitterness, witchcraft, and idolatry. She also had a murderous spirit. Nothing would stop her from getting what she wanted.

First Kings 21:4–7 clearly reveals how the couple–one inward, one outward—linked together to form a double-minded union and accomplish wicked things:

> Ahab returned home angry and depressed because of the answer Naboth the Jezreelite had given him, for he had said, "I will not give you the inheritance of my fathers." He lay down on his bed and sulked and would not eat any bread.
>
> But Jezebel his wife came to him and said, "Why is your spirit so sad that you refuse to eat bread?"
>
> And he said to her, "Because I spoke to Naboth the Jezreelite and said to him, 'Give me your vineyard for money; or else, if you prefer, I will give you another vineyard for it.' And he answered, 'I will not give you my vineyard.'"

> Jezebel his wife said to him, "Are you not the governor of the kingdom of Israel? Get up and eat bread, and let your heart be happy, for I will get the vineyard of Naboth the Jezreelite for you."

Ahab would pout in rejection, and Jezebel would rise up to retaliate in rebellion. Together they advanced wicked plots in Israel, driving the country to being rejected by God, led into bondage, and left in desolated ruins. This is what the rejection and rebellion personalities accomplish when they work together within double-mindedness. They cannot be allowed to link up. In order to be disarmed, they must be separated and then cast out of the double-minded person.

God came in and delivered Israel from Ahab and Jezebel's diabolical rule. He unlinked their association with one another. They needed each other and drew strength from each other. Jezebel could not do what she did without Ahab. The spirit of Jezebel entered Israel through this marriage, and she brought in Baal worship. Ahab also used Jezebel's manipulation and control to do his dirty work. They worked together just as Ida Mae Hammond saw in her revelation of rejection and rebellion. She saw the double-minded bondage as two hands clenched together with the fingers crossing over each other. These hands need to be pulled apart and the fingers separated in order to destroy this stronghold.[5]

The Jezebel spirit is domineering, manipulative, and seductive. It intimidates, threatens, lies, and does whatever it takes to accomplish its end. Jezebel had Naboth killed in order to possess his vineyard for her husband. She also murdered the prophets of God and threatened Elijah's life. The Jezebel spirit is vengeful and vindictive, evil and wicked. There is no peace while this spirit is active:

> When Joram saw Jehu he said, "Is it peace, Jehu?" And he said, "What peace, so long as the harlotries of your mother Jezebel and her sorceries are so many?"
>
> —2 KINGS 9:22

Rebellion is a wicked personality that needs to be renounced and cast out. We will remain in bondage to it until we see how wicked it is.

The Ahab spirit is lustful, weak, and fearful, and tolerates wickedness. King Ahab allowed Jezebel to bring in the worship of Baal. His spirit is passive and will not stand up for righteousness. This inward and withdrawn personality is also wicked and needs to be renounced and cast out. God hates rejection just as He hates rebellion.

> Ahab said to Elijah, "Have you found me, my enemy?" And he answered, "I have found you, because you have sold yourself to work evil in the sight of the LORD. 'See, I will bring disaster upon you and will take away your posterity and will cut off all your males, both free and slave, who are left in Israel, and will make your house like the house of Jeroboam the son of Nebat and like the house of Baasha the son of Ahijah, for the provocation with which you have provoked Me to anger and made Israel to sin.'"
>
> —1 KINGS 21:20–22

God judged the house of Ahab for its wickedness. Ahab was idolatrous, compromising, lustful, covetous, and weak. He was a rejected man who was connected to a rebellious woman.

Ruthless, murderous, treacherous, idolatrous, seductive, controlling, intimidating, and wicked, Jezebel was also judged by God for her wickedness. Her path ended with dogs eating up her flesh. (See 2 Kings 9.)

In his book *Spiritual Warfare* Richard Ing summarizes the two perfectly. He says:

> Ahab men are double-minded compromisers. In 1 Kings chapter twenty, the powerful Syrian army twice came against Israel. Both times a prophet of God came to Ahab and told him that God was going to give a mighty miracle to Ahab and defeat the Syrians. God indeed routed the Syrians twice. Still, Ahab did not return to worshipping God. Yet, he inquired of God's prophets when he wanted help (1 Kings 22:6). He went back and forth—truly a double-minded man. Ahab men go to church if it is politically correct or for personal gain, not because they love God. They witness God's miracles and still refuse to come to the Lord.
>
> Jezebel is a witch by definition and action. Witchcraft is manipulation and control of others through demonic means. She seeks to control the minds of others through lies, complaining, threats, position, shame, pity, and whatever else she can use.[6]

As you have been praying and reading through this chapter, if you have found that you exhibit Ahab-like qualities, ask the Lord to reveal to you any alliances with Jezebel spirits. Those are ungodly soul ties that must be broken in order for you to experience deliverance from the Ahab spirit. There is no shame in coming for deliverance and prayer, though the enemy loves to keep us from owning up to the spiritual oppression the Lord reveals to us. But I encourage you to be bold in this area and to be relentless as you seek to destroy the influence of this spirit.

Rejection and the Criminal Mind

People who have served prison time for criminal activity (especially violent crimes) will need deliverance after being released. Many churches are not equipped to minister to ex-offenders because there is a lack of teaching and training in deliverance. There is also a lack of revelation in the area of double-mindedness.

I have a teaching series on double-mindedness (it is available on my website). Included in this teaching is my revelation of the deliverance needs for what I have termed "criminal schizophrenia" or "criminal double-mindedness." People with a history of criminal activity are usually in need of deliverance from double-mindedness. The rebellion personality in the double-minded includes spirits of bitterness, violence, murder, retaliation, lawlessness, and anti-submissiveness. These spirits are also connected to rejection.

Ex-criminals experience a compounded form of rejection brought on by societal rejection. Convicted felons have a difficult time acclimating back into life once they are released back into society. They also have a difficult time staying faithful to Christ because of double-mindedness, which will often cause them to go back into criminal activity. They need acceptance and love from a church community that understands deliverance and the double-minded personality. Such a community of believers can help this individual stay free, never to return to a life of crime. Can you imagine how much a Spirit-filled, Bible-believing, prophetic church could impact the rate of repeat offenders? Prison ministry is a deliverance ministry.

Rejection and Arrested Development

Sometimes people who have been rejected, especially early in life, get stuck mentally and emotionally at the time the first significant rejection experience occurred. Many times they remain childlike in their understanding of life, in processing emotions, and in their behavior toward others, often being selfish and self-centered. It is as if they have been frozen in time. This is called arrested development. It operates in a specific area of the mind, targeting regression from ages thirteen to zero. For every year to which it causes a person to regress, a different spirit manifests. There is a different demon assigned to each age, and each (age) demon has a specific task.

As it operates in reverse, this spirit's main objective is to hinder a person's spiritual and natural growth. It aims to take the person back to the position in the womb and choke him to death. Many people who experience choking in their sleep may be struggling with this spirit. Even if its task is not completed, arrested development opens the door for spirits of terror by night, nightmares (controlled by a demon named Mare), and fear of the dark.

The arrested development spirit wants to embarrass a person at all times by manifesting the different age personalities, thus making a person's immature words or advice an accepted reality, causing him to doubt his own ability to make mature decisions.

This spirit also works with double-mindedness and spirits of homosexuality and lesbianism. This demon may try to create designs for a person's life by setting up events of rape and incest and by allowing spirits of rejection, homosexuality, hurt, fear, double-mindedness, inability to give or receive love, isolation, and hatred of men or women to enter the person's life.

Many people who are bound by this spirit find that they try to escape hardship in life by turning to drugs and alcohol. It works strongly with Ahab, Jezebel, and whoredom spirits to keep people depressed over their lives, forcing them to regress to happier childhood years, while attempting to keep them from developing mentally.

First Corinthians 13:11 says, "When I was a child, I spoke as a child, I understood as a child, and I thought as a child. But when I became a man, I put away childish things."

There are three states in which the spirit of arrested development tries to keep the person:

1. Speaking as a child
2. Understanding as a child
3. Thinking as a child

The Word of God teaches us the power of the spoken word—death and life are in the power of the tongue (Prov. 18:21). In his letter to the Corinthians Paul separates and distinguishes the things spoken by children and those spoken by adults. As mature saints we are to speak with the wisdom (mature things) of the Word. In Hebrews 5:12–14 we see that our understanding is to be matured.

Left unchallenged, the spirit of arrested development will stop a person from maturing past childhood. Adults who still play with toys and collect dolls are manifesting the characteristics of children. This could be the spirit of arrested development manifesting through fantasy and escape of reality, other spirits that come out of rejection.

Through arrested development and the other demonic manifestations discussed in this chapter, we are gaining a clearer picture of how the spirit of rejection desolates the human soul, leaving a person fragmented and in pieces. Controlled by this spirit, people are left unable to be their true selves—the selves that God created to showcase His glory. There is no call, purpose, or destiny that can be sustained while a person is controlled by this demon.

CHAPTER 4

FEAR AND PARANOIA

Fear and trembling come into me, and horror has overwhelmed me.

—PSALM 55:5

FEAR OFTEN MANIFESTS itself in everyday life as procrastination and indecision. While many people will openly admit to having issues with procrastination or indecision, they may not be aware that these two issues are directly linked to fear of rejection, fear of the future, fear of failure, and fear of making decisions, either good or bad.

Fear is a paralyzing spirit that keeps people bound in many areas of their lives. This spirit manifests itself in numerous ways: fear of rejection (works with rejection and self-rejection), fear of abandonment, fear of hurt, fear of authority (including pastors), fear of witchcraft, fear of career, fear of dying, fear of failure, fear of the future, fear of responsibility, fear of darkness, fear of being alone, fear of what people think or say about you, fear of hell, fear of demons and deliverance, fear of poverty, fear of germs, fear of marriage, fear of dogs, fear of accidents, fear of man, fear of Jezebel, fear of confrontation, fear of poverty, and more.

Phobias are extreme fears that freeze a person to inaction. Panic, panic attacks, terror, fright, apprehension, sudden fear, and more are expressions of that. Talkativeness, nervousness, worry, anxiety, and tension can also be manifestations of the fear cluster of demons.

Fear Can Lead to Paranoia

Paranoia is a cluster of demons rooted in fear and is one of the stronger manifestations of the rejection personality. Paranoia blames others and is suspicious of them without reason. It causes a person to question the motives of others and judges them without having any basis for doing so. It is rooted in fear and rejection.

King Saul presented a classic case of paranoia in his suspicion of those around him, especially David. In 1 Samuel 22:8 he accused them of conspiring to take his kingdom, saying, "You have all conspired against me, and no one revealed to me that my son made a covenant with the son of Jesse. And not one of you is grieved for me and revealed it to me that my son raised up my servant against me to ambush me as at this day." We see the same self-pity and poutiness that we witnessed in King Ahab when Saul said that that no one felt sorry for him.

Most likely the people who heard him talk like this were confused. Targets of a double-minded person's suspicions are often perplexed when their motives are judged for no reason. The suspicions arise out of the person's delusions and are not based in reality, which is the case of what happened with Saul.

> When they came home, as David was returning from slaying the Philistine, the women came out from all cities of Israel to meet King Saul, singing and dancing, with tambourines, with joy, and with musical instruments. The dancing women sang and said, "Saul has slain his thousands, and David his ten thousands."
>
> Saul became very angry, and this saying was displeasing

> to him. Therefore he said, "They have ascribed to David ten thousands, but to me they have ascribed thousands. Now what remains for him to have but the kingdom?" So Saul was suspicious of David from that day and forward.
>
> —1 Samuel 18:6–9

David had done nothing to deserve Saul's suspicion. He had been faithful to Saul. Like all double-minded leaders, Saul needed deliverance. By using or abusing their power and authority, leaders who are suspicious of everyone around them will do all they can to destroy the targets of their suspicion. Saul eventually tried to murder David.

Have you ever been around someone who was suspicious of everyone? Such individuals think everyone is out to get them. They don't trust anyone. This can be a sign of instability and double-mindedness.

Saul's fear ultimately led him to disobedience, rejection by God, and being removed as king over Israel:

> Samuel said, "Does the Lord delight in burnt offerings and sacrifices as much as in obeying the voice of the Lord? Obedience is better than sacrifice, a listening ear than the fat of rams. For rebellion is as the sin of witchcraft, and stubbornness is as iniquity and idolatry. Because you have rejected the word of the Lord, He has also rejected you from being king."
>
> Saul said to Samuel, "I have sinned. For I have transgressed the commandment of the Lord, and your words, because I feared the people, and obeyed their voice. Now therefore, please pardon my sin and return with me, that I may worship the Lord."
>
> Samuel said to Saul, "I will not return with you. For you have rejected the word of the Lord, and the Lord has rejected you from being king over Israel."
>
> —1 Samuel 15:22–26

OTHER BIBLICAL REFERENCES TO THE SPIRIT OF FEAR

Fear is an unpleasant and often strong emotion caused by an anticipation or awareness of danger; dread, fright, or alarm in the presence of others. Fear is one of Satan's greatest weapons against the believer. It is the opposite of faith, and faith is what we need in order to be pleasing to God.

People raised in an atmosphere without love (i.e., rejection, strife, violence, etc.) usually have many spirits of fear. Some biblical references to fear include:[1]

- Apollyon (Rev. 9:11)—ruling spirit of fear, death, and destruction
- Scorpion spirits of fear that cause torment (Rev. 9:1–11)
- Emim (Deut. 2:10–11)—a giant, warlike race; the word in Hebrew means terrible ones"[2]
- Fear of death (Ps. 55:4)
- Hittites—one of the tribes inhabiting the land of Canaan who were to be driven out by the Israelites; *Hittite* refers to breaking in pieces, sundering, dismay, terror, and dread[3]
- Rephaim (Gen. 15:20)—the giants, meaning gloom, terrors, fears, fearful ones, strong ones
- Spirit of bondage (Rom. 8:15)—causes fear, which can result in backsliding, loss of salvation, and so on
- Sudden fear (Prov. 3:25)

Phobias—Intense Fear

A phobia is "intense fear of certain situations, activities, things, animals, or people."[4] Usually triggered in childhood around the age of thirteen for most as a result of emotional or physical trauma, "phobias are the most common type of emotional disorders in the US. They are a type of anxiety disorder, which is the most prevalent mental disorder."[5] Please understand that these phobias are inordinate, crippling fears that interrupt a person's ability to carry on normal living. Phobias should not be accepted as a way of life. Anything that keeps us from enjoying a good and godly life needs to be dealt with. Deliverance, prayer ministry, and counseling can help a person to begin to regain authority in an area that has been ravaged by intense, paralyzing fear.

You can use the list below to help you to identify the fears you are tormented by; use their proper names when you renounce their power over your life. If the phobia that torments you is not listed, you can check out the more complete list at www.phobiasource.com/phobia-list. You may also find that you are not strong enough to face these demons of fear on your own, so solicit the help of a mature minister to help you destroy the spirit of fear and panic.

> For God has not given us the spirit of fear, but of power, and love, and self-control.
>
> —2 Timothy 1:7

- Acrophobia—fear of heights
- Agliophobia—fear of pain
- Agrizoophobia—fear of wild animals
- Anthropophobia—fear of people or society

- Aquaphobia—fear of water
- Arachnephobia—fear of spiders
- Ataxophobia—fear of disorder or untidiness
- Atychiphobia—fear of failure
- Autophobia—fear of being alone
- Aviophobia—fear of flying
- Cenophobia—fear of new things or ideas
- Chiraptophobia—fear of being touched
- Claustrophobia—fear of confined spaces
- Cynophobia—fear of dogs or rabies
- Decidophobia—fear of making decisions
- Demonophobia—fear of demons
- Dentophobia—fear of dentists
- Dystychiphobia—fear of accidents
- Ecclesiophobia—fear of church
- Elurophobia—fear of cats
- Entomophobia—fear of insects
- Glossophobia—fear of speaking in public or of trying to speak
- Hadephobia—fear of hell
- Hamartophobia—fear of sinning
- Hexakosioihexekontahexaphobia—fear of the number 666

- Mysophobia—fear of being contaminated with dirt or germs
- Noctiphobia—fear of the night
- Nosocomephobia—fear of hospitals
- Obesophobia—fear of gaining weight
- Panophobia—fear of everything
- Peniaphobia—fear of poverty
- Pharmacophobia—fear of taking medicine
- Philophobia—fear of falling in love or being in love
- Somniphobia—fear of sleep
- Tocophobia—fear of pregnancy or childbirth
- Tropophobia—fear of making changes
- Xenophobia—fear of strangers or foreigners[6]

Fear, paranoia, intimidation, and phobias are some of the most debilating issues of a human heart. Fear can cause isolation and fits of panic that can lead to violence. Fear can keep a person from living life altogether. It keeps people from living to their full potential and experiencing success. People who live with fear, worry, and anxiety also live with great regret, wishing they had the courage and boldness to do the things God wants them to do. Fear can keep a person from believing God for healing and restoration. When Jesus healed the sick, He told them that it was their faith that made them whole (Mark 5:34). Fearful people live in constant doubt and faithlessness. The Bible says that what does not come from faith is sin (Rom. 14:23). So we definitely want to break the power of fear over our lives so that we can walk in faith and experience godly success.

CHAPTER 5

THE KINGDOM OF PERVERSION

Those who are of a perverse heart are abomination to the Lord*,*
but such as are upright in their way are His delight.

—Proverbs 11:20

In Hebrews 4:12–13 the Bible says, "For the word of God is alive, and active, and sharper than any two-edged sword, piercing even to the division of soul and spirit, of joints and marrow, and able to judge [or discern] the thoughts and intents of the heart. There is no creature that is not revealed in His sight, for all things are bare and exposed to the eyes of Him to whom we must give account."

Notice that this verse refers to the Word of God functioning as "a discerner of the thoughts and intents of the heart" (kjv). What this is basically saying is that the more of the Word of God you know, the more discernment you will operate in. When you are flowing in discernment, the enemy cannot hide from you. There are three realms of discernment: 1) an impartation of the gift of discerning of spirits by the Holy Spirit, 2) discernment developed through spiritual experience, 3) and discernment by way of the Word of God.

Look again at Hebrews 4:13: "There is no creature that is not revealed in His sight." Whose sight? The Word of God. Jesus is the Word of God made flesh (John 1:1–14). Nothing can hide from the Word. No creature can hide from the Word, "for all things are bare and exposed to the eyes of Him to whom we must give account." The Word is able to manifest, expose, make naked, and open our eyes to the creatures that try to hide.

In dealing with demons, we're dealing with creatures. Demons are beings created by God. At one time they lived in heaven with God, but now they are fallen angels who rebelled against God. The creature is not greater than the Creator. Satan and his kingdom are made up of nothing more than creatures. Satan is not God. He wants to be, but he isn't.

Notice that every creature is exposed through the Word of God, including demons and devils. This is what we are doing in this book; we are using the Word of God to expose the spirit of rejection. It will not remain hidden in your life. It will be revealed in the sight of God. It will be exposed, made naked, and destroyed. The Spirit of God can show you how and where this spirit is at work in your life.

In this chapter we are going to expose another stronghold that operates within the spirit of rejection—perversion. Pulling down the strongholds that have set up demonic chains in your life is the key to being delivered from the stubborn demon of rejection.

If you recall, we discussed in the introduction and in chapter 1 that people take on rejection through trauma and abuse. As a result of rejection that enters a life through sexual abuse, molestation, incest, and rape (especially if these happen in childhood), an individual can become open to a spirit of perversion. The Bible says in Hebrews 12:15–17:

> Watching diligently so that no one falls short of the grace of God, lest any root of bitterness spring up to cause trouble, and many become defiled by it, lest there be any sexually

> immoral or profane person, as Esau, who for one morsel of food sold his birthright. For you know that afterward, when he wanted to inherit the blessing, he was rejected. For he found no place of repentance, though he sought it diligently with tears.

Notice that one of the root problems people have, sometimes as a result of the hurts or trauma they may have experienced, is called a root of bitterness. When bitterness is in your heart, it can lead you directly into sexual immorality. When you have unresolved hurts—anger, rejection, bitterness, unforgiveness, resentment, and so on—the devil attempts to drive you into sexual sin. He often starts by causing rejection to come into your life when you are at a very young age.

Some may say, "I don't care what people think about me." Yes, you do. Rejection hurts. We all want to be loved and accepted—and we should be. The pain of rejection can become so consuming that finding any way to cover up or to escape the pain is all our souls and spirits want to do. Rejection causes an insatiable desire to be loved and accepted while still holding on to the fear that one is unlovable and will never be accepted. (You can see how even in rejection a person exhibits a level of double-mindedness that can only come from the demonic realm. God is not the author of confusion [1 Cor. 14:33].) The rejected personality seeks love and attention many times through ungodly connections that include perverse behavior and sexual sin.

In chapter 3 I mentioned that perversion doesn't come alone; it comes with a cluster of demons, including homosexuality, lesbianism, fetishes, molestation, and other sexual impurities such as pornography, masturbation, fantasy, incest, pedophilia, sodomy, adultery, fornication, whoredom, harlotry, and seduction. I call this demonic cluster the kingdom of perversion.

In some cases when people come for deliverance, they are dealing with more than just demons. They are dealing with kingdoms that Satan has set up in their lives. The driving motivation of a kingdom is to rally behind a king to establish rule over a territory. Demonic kingdoms are set up in the spirit realm much as natural kingdoms are set up—with a king whose army has generals, captains, lieutenants, and other ranks and officials. In the demonic realm we are not just dealing with one little isolated demon. We see that this is very true when we start to dismantle the spirit of rejection and find that the kingdom of perversion has tried to set up camp in a person's life. Let's take a closer look and bring the operation of this kingdom to light.

Perversion Is a Heart Issue

> Because, although they knew God, they did not glorify Him or give thanks to Him as God, but became futile in their imaginations, and their foolish hearts were darkened. Claiming to be wise, they became fools. They changed the glory of the incorruptible God into an image made like corruptible man, birds, four-footed beasts, and creeping things. Therefore God gave them up to uncleanness through the lusts of their hearts, to dishonor their own bodies among themselves. They turned the truth of God into a lie and worshipped and served the creature rather than the Creator, who is blessed forever. Amen.
>
> —Romans 1:21–25

Notice in verse 21 that God zeros in on the heart. The spirit of perversion is a heart issue. There are many today who are preaching that certain lifestyles listed in Romans 1, such as homosexuality, are just nature, things that can't change.

Regarding homosexuality, it was even proposed for a while that there might be a gene that ties it to heredity and causes one to be predisposed to being homosexual or transgender. And some are teaching that if you are a homosexual or have a leaning toward that lifestyle, there is no use trying to change because that's who you are and you can't change. There are homosexuals who have tried to change and found themselves right back in a homosexual lifestyle.

Homosexuality is a stubborn demon to break free from. Often women and men think that if they marry a person of the opposite sex, their problem with homosexuality will go away. But they bring this problem into the marriage. They may be faithful to a mate for a period of time, but then they find themselves back in homosexual relationships that can eventually destroy the marriage.

The same can be said for fornication and adultery. All of these behaviors are attached to this kingdom of perversion. One is not cleaner than the other. They are all abominations to God, and they all have the same issues that reside in the heart.

Fornication

The term *fornication*—from the Greek word *porneia,* which is where we get our English word *pornography*—is defined as "illicit sexual intercourse: adultery, fornication, homosexuality, lesbianism, intercourse with animals etc.; sexual intercourse with close relatives (Lev. 18); sexual intercourse with a divorced man or woman (Mk. 10:11, 12)."[1] *Fornication* is a general term for sexual sin. When the Bible says to avoid fornication, it is referring to sexual sin of all types: lust, adultery, homosexuality, lesbianism, bisexuality, pedophilia, incest, and so on.

Fornication is a condition of the heart. If you try to change an ungodly sexual lifestyle without dealing with your heart, you are doomed to failure. These things do not come from the outside; they come from the inside. The things that we do with our bodies don't come from our bodies; they come from our hearts.

If you are struggling with sexual sin, know that there is something inside of you that needs to be dealt with. All sin originates in the heart. So if you're struggling with homosexuality, lesbianism, adultery, pornography, or any other type of sexual sin, and you have tried to repent, have come for deliverance, have come against the powers of darkness, and have declared, "I'm not going to do this anymore," but you haven't dealt with your heart, you'll never get victory over these areas. God has to do a work inside your heart.

Often when the Holy Spirit is invited to search inside and examine the heart, there is more than just fornication present. Bitterness, envy, fear, jealousy, and rejection also show up. These are things in the heart that cause you to get involved in sexual sin. This is why it is so important that every believer does the following three things:

1. Receive the gift of salvation
2. Be filled with the Holy Spirit
3. Receive deliverance

You have to allow God to cleanse your heart. You have to make sure you are serving God with a pure heart. So if there is something in your life that you keep getting into over and over, you need to look at your heart. You need to ask the Lord to reveal what is in your heart that may be causing you to fall again and again. Without the help of the Holy Spirit you won't know what's in you.

> Search me, O God, and know my heart; try me, and know my concerns, and see if there is any rebellious way in me, and lead me in the ancient way.
>
> —Psalm 139:23–24

Demons That Operate in the Kingdom of Perversion

> And since they did not see fit to acknowledge God, God gave them over to a debased mind, to do those things which are not proper. They were filled with all unrighteousness, sexual immorality, wickedness, covetousness, maliciousness; full of envy, murder, strife, deceit. They are gossips, slanderers, God-haters, insolent, proud, boastful, inventors of evil things, and disobedient toward parents, without understanding, covenant breakers, without natural affection, calloused, and unmerciful.
>
> —Romans 1:28–31

You can be full of the Holy Spirit, as it says in Ephesians 5:18, but you can also be full of demons, as the passage above states. People who reject God invite the kingdom of perversion to take up occupancy in their lives, filling them with "all unrighteousness" and everything that follows. When a person is oppressed by the spirit of perversion, these are the demonic spirits that infiltrate his or her life:

Unrighteousness

Unrighteousness means sinfulness, wickedness, and injustice. The Bible says all unrighteousness is sin (1 John 5:17, KJV).

Sexual immorality (or "fornication," in the King James Version)

As we have seen already, we know that the Greek word meaning "fornication" is *porneia,* which is where we get the word *pornography.* Fornication is more than two unmarried people coming together sexually; it is the umbrella term for all sexual sin and impurity.

Wickedness

Wickedness, like fornication, is another umbrella term. According to Webster's dictionary, *wicked* is defined as "morally very bad: evil; fierce, vicious; disgustingly unpleasant: vile; causing or likely to cause harm, distress, or trouble."[2] In the Bible wickedness is characterized as the spirit of Belial, which is the ruling spirit of wickedness. Mentioned in the Bible sixteen times, Belial is responsible for spirits such as idolatry, uncleanness, Jezebel, rape and sexual abuse, alcoholism and drunkenness, infirmity, pornography, wicked plots, antichrist, seared conscience, lack of thoughtfulness, unloving, inconsiderate, and ungodly soul ties. I provide a more thorough look into this spirit in my book *Deliverance and Spiritual Warfare Manual.*

Covetousness

Webster's defines *covetous,* the adjective form of *covetousness,* as "feeling or showing a very strong desire for something that you do not have and especially for something that belongs to someone else."[3] Covetousness is about being dissatisfied with what you have, and it often gives place to jealousy, envy, and even murder. It is interesting that Romans 1:21 says, "Although they knew God, they did not glorify Him or give thanks to Him as God." As a believer I find it hard to fathom that someone can know God and not give Him glory and thanks, even if it's just for who He is. He doesn't even have to do anything to cause some of us to thank Him. But a person who is tormented by covetousness is not satisfied or content; most of all they are not thankful. They are always thinking they deserve or should have more than what they do.

It's also interesting to note that ungratefulness is one of the things that opens the door to the kingdom of perversion. We have too many gripers and complainers today, especially in America. America is the most blessed, fattest, most gluttonous nation on the planet. We throw away more food than some people have to eat in a whole year. We drive good cars. But if we don't have everything we think we should have or if someone doesn't give it to us how and when we want it, we complain. We're not thankful. And according to Romans 1, this is the first step to leaving God.

You need to thank God for the blessings that you have. Thank Him for the sun, moon, and stars. Thank Him for the rain and the sunshine. Thank Him for letting you live and not die. Thank Him for waking you up this morning. Don't be like the people in Romans 1:21 who knew God but didn't give Him glory. You don't want to be the one whom God gave up to all kinds of wickedness and evil. You don't want God to say to you, "Because you have rejected My knowledge, I will reject you."

No matter what you go through in life, keep praising and worshipping God. Don't let anything, anybody, any devil, and any demon stop you from praising and worshipping God, because when it's all over, He is still good!

Thanksgiving and gratitude can rescue you out of a pit of despair and is a remedy for covetousness. Thanksgiving is something God wants you to always have. You should always thank God for your blessings.

An ungrateful heart can also be a sign of arrogance. You should never get to the place where you think it was you that got you where you are today. If it were not for the mercy of God, you'd be a mess. You'd be lost. You'd be in sin. You'd be in hell!

When you take for granted the blessings of heaven, then you start saying that there's no God. When you stop thanking God, you become vain and empty, having no substance. You'll become vain in your imaginations, your foolish heart will darken, and just when you think you're so smart and wise, you become a fool.

The Bible says, "The fool has said in his heart, 'There is no God'" (Ps. 14:1). When you begin to believe that there is no God, that He doesn't deserve honor and praise, and that you don't have to submit to Him—and this is the kind of thing being said today—you have become a fool. And when you become a fool, you'll do anything.

Fools do things that cause them to self-destruct. This is where the spirit of destruction comes in again. This is where we begin to see the manifestation of a reprobate mind. A fool will keep on drinking alcohol even after a doctor tells him he is going to die. A fool will keep smoking even when the doctor tells him he's going to get lung cancer. Fools do things that don't make sense. Fools do things that are counterproductive. Fools make unwise decisions. Fools ruin their own lives and then blame it on someone else. This is the downward spiral of the unthankful, unsatisfied heart of a covetous person. Such a person does not give God the praise that is due Him.

Maliciousness

Demons by nature are malicious. *Malicious* comes from the word *malice*, which means "desire to cause pain, injury, or distress to another."[4] Malicious people want to see others suffer, especially if the individuals did them wrong, didn't give them their way, or won't let them be in control. A malicious person has a desire to see such an individual hurt.

Envy

We're not talking about a little spirit of envy in the corner. We're not talking about one little demon hiding up under the table somewhere. Roman 1:29 says "full of envy." This can also refer to jealousy, covetousness, and unthankfulness. It is the "painful or resentful awareness of an advantage enjoyed by another joined with a desire to possess the same advantage."[5]

Murder

This demon enters through hatred, anger, and bitterness. In Matthew 5:21–22 Jesus said, "You have heard that it was said by the ancients, 'You shall not murder,' and 'Whoever murders shall be in danger of the judgment.' But I say to you that whoever is angry with his brother without a cause shall be in danger of the judgment." Again, by His being the Word made flesh, Jesus was full of discernment. All the demonic spirits, such as murder, that attach themselves to anger and bitterness could not hide from Him. He then took on a prophetic mantle and exposed their connection to us so that we could loose ourselves from their grip.

Strife

Strife refers to those who like to debate, argue, and stir up discord and disagreement. Some people always want to argue and never want to hear someone else's perspective. This spirit also keeps individuals from hearing the truth about themselves and where they need to be with God.

If you are saved, then you know that the main part of your receiving salvation was first admitting you were wrong and then repenting. You couldn't come in arguing with the preacher: "I don't really need to be saved. I don't have to read my Bible. I don't have to belong to this church. I can be what I want to be." Then when you're confronted with the truth of God's Word, the demon of strife would have you say, "Well, I don't believe that. That's your interpretation." No. You knew that in order to receive salvation, you had to come into agreement with the Word of God.

If the Bible says, "Thou shalt not suffer a witch to live," how many ways can you interpret that? If it says, "Homosexuality is an abomination; it disgusts God," how many ways can you interpret that? You don't have to have a PhD to understand that. But people want to debate.

If you have ever wondered what's wrong with people who always argue with the Bible, then know that they are dealing with this spirit of strife. Be careful because people will have you arguing about stuff that doesn't even make sense as far as eternity is concerned. Do not entertain this spirit.

Deceit

This is the spirit of deception. It includes deceiving spirits such as cunning, lying, and manipulation.

Gossip

This demon is one of the spirits of the tongue, which also include slander and negative, divisive talking.

Slander

Slander is another spirit that influences the tongue, or what we say. It includes lying, gossip, lying about another person (false witness), criticism, and the like.

God-haters

Unfortunately we are seeing a lot of this in our American culture. Many people would like to shut down the name of Jesus. We've taken prayer out of schools. We've begun to call preaching the truth of the Word of God "hate speech." Today it seems that everyone is tolerant of everything except the things of God.

Insolence

This is another spirit that influences our speech. The adjective form *insolent* means "insultingly contemptuous in speech or conduct: overbearing."[6] It also means "rude or impolite: having or showing a lack of respect for other people."[7]

Pride

Pride is a stubborn demon that is often the most difficult to dislodge from a person's life. It is personified in Job 41 as Leviathan. You will always find this spirit in a kingdom somewhere. Pride is also related to arrogance, haughtiness, and superiority. The Pharisees were examples of the spirit of pride, which manifested itself as a religious spirit. We'll talk more about this spirit in the next chapter.

Boastful

This spirit is related closely to pride. It can also be a spirit that influences the tongue, or what we say. Boasting is not only about feeling pride or superior but also about reinforcing that feeling with bragging. The Bible says that God has chosen the foolish things of the world to confound the wise so that no man can boast. (See 1 Corinthians 1:27.) God favors and blesses the humble, but He resists the proud. The proud and boastful do not receive help from the Lord.

Inventors of evil things

Now more than ever people are thinking of new ways to do evil. With no regard for God, wisdom, or anything prudent, people are coming with more ways to oppress, torture, and manipulate others. Our news media are flooded with the actions of groups like ISIS and Boko Haram killing women and children and forcing people from their homes. In the United States, through the rise of abortion and same-sex advocacy, we are seeing new ways for people to use political systems, violence, and terrorism to promote evil.

Disobedience to parents

The Bible says in Ephesians 6:1–3, "Children, obey your parents in the Lord, for this is right. 'Honor your father and mother,' which is the first commandment with a promise, 'so that it may be well with you and you may live long on the earth.'" It is not well with many of our young people today, though some would like to say that it is mom and dad's fault. There is a growing disrespect for authority among youth. Many shows on television promote a distrust and disrespect of authority. Many times parents, especially fathers, are pictured as clueless, out of touch, and just plain dumb. I have already pointed out some of the rejection that is at the root of many of the issues we are seeing in our youth, especially when it comes to the spirit of perversion.

What many young people are not being taught is that, no matter what, God still has a blessing and promise for those who honor and obey their parents as unto the Lord. Parents are not perfect, and in some extreme cases it takes a lot of deliverance and help to develop the discernment and strategy to honor parents who may be abusive or under the influence of the spirits of rejection or perversion themselves.

God will honor those who honor their parents. Rebellion against parents opens the door for a young person to be afflicted with many demons.

Without understanding

People who lack understanding say things such as: "I don't understand why that's wrong." "I don't understand why I'll go to hell if I do that." "I don't understand why I have to give that up." Well, of course they don't. They are without understanding.

The devil will block your understanding. You will be blind and in the dark. You'll be so mixed up and confused until you won't even understand who you are. The Bible says, "Wisdom is principal; therefore get wisdom. And with all your getting, get understanding" (Prov. 4:7). You need wisdom *and* understanding.

Covenant breakers

People who are involved in perversion jump in and out of relationships as if it's nothing. There is no faithfulness or loyalty in relationships. People who are struggling with adultery, fornication, homosexuality, lesbianism, and bisexuality have gone to bed with many different people. They do not keep covenant.

Without natural affection

This phrase in the Greek means "unloving" and "devoid of affection." It means "hard-hearted toward kindred," or having no love, compassion, empathy, or affection for those in your own family or community.[8]

Implacable

This means that someone you are dealing with won't be appeased, compromised with, placated, or satisfied. You can't make truces or peace with them.

Unmerciful

"Blessed are the merciful, for they shall obtain mercy" (Matt. 5:7). People who are controlled by perversion have no mercy or compassion. They are just cruel and selfish. Until they turn from this and repent, they will receive no mercy or compassion from God. Remember, as indicated in the ministry of Christ while He was on the earth, compassion is what drives God to intervene in our lives to bring great deliverance, healing, and breakthrough.

These are the demonic spirits that operate in the kingdom of perversion. In Romans 1 the apostle Paul is talking about men and women who would not worship God and got wrapped up in perversion (lesbianism and homosexuality). As a result, God turned them over to those desires and they became reprobate. Their minds became opened to all these demons to come in.

If you or someone you are praying for or ministering to has perverse spirits, you can use this list from Romans 1 as a guide for calling out each of these spirits. They will manifest and the person will get tremendous deliverance. Above all, be led by the Spirit of God. Don't be bound by this list, but use it as a reference point to become familiar with these demonic spirits. Then the Holy Spirit will bring back to your remembrance these things when you are called on to minister to someone.

GUARD YOUR HEART

> For out of the heart proceed evil thoughts, murders, adulteries, sexual immorality, thefts, false witness, and blasphemies. These are the things which defile a man. But to eat with unwashed hands does not defile a man.
>
> —MATTHEW 15:19–20

As I have said, the spirit of perversion rises out of the heart. Homosexuality, lesbianism, adultery, and fornication are all heart issues. If you are a practicing homosexual, no matter how much you defend your lifestyle, you have a heart issue. Somehow the enemy was able to plant the seed in your heart through trauma whether by direct means (such as molestation) or by indirect means (such as generational trauma). Because you did not guard your heart—or weren't spiritually equipped to guard your heart—the seed grew and manifested as perversion.

Let me give you an example. If a man molests a young boy, the boy may grow up with homosexual tendencies because his heart was open. He didn't know how to close his heart to that.

Now, you can close your heart to things. You can make a decision, "I'm not going to be a homosexual." You can shut your heart to it and say, "No, I will not be gay. I hate it. I don't want to be a homosexual." You can make a decision at a young age not to be a homosexual. There are a lot of men who were molested at a young age and could have been homosexuals, but they said no to it. When you close your heart to the defilement of the enemy, there is nothing the devil can do to get it in your heart.

Proverbs 4:23 says, "Keep your heart with all diligence, for out of it are the issues of life." What comes into your life flows out of your heart. How you end up in life is based on how you keep your heart. You end up in certain places because of what came out of your heart. Judas, a disciple of Jesus, is an example of what happens when you don't guard your heart.

> Now supper being concluded, the devil had put into the heart of Judas Iscariot, Simon's son, to betray Him.
>
> —John 13:2

Not only do we see that Judas's heart was open to the enemy, but we also learn something about Satan. He likes to put things in the heart. He'll put the thoughts in your mind and inclinations into your heart: "You're a homosexual. You're a lesbian. Because you allowed this molestation to happen, you must like it. You must be homosexual. How else can you explain it?" If you receive these lies as truth, they will get in your heart and you will act them out.

All sexual sin begins with a thought. You just don't fall in the bed with somebody. You think about it before it happens. You don't wake up saying, "What? What happened? How did I get here?" It begins with a thought.

You will never get victory over sexual sin until you take authority over the way you think. I don't care how much deliverance you receive; you have to control your thoughts. You can't think about sexual sin, meditate on it, and then expect not to get involved in it. The more you think about something, the greater the chances are that you'll end up doing it.

We must take our thoughts captive as 2 Corinthians 10:5 says: "Casting down imaginations and every high thing that exalts itself against the knowledge of God, bringing every thought into captivity to the obedience of Christ." A lot of us are just too lazy. We let the devil run around in our minds all day long, from the moment we get up to the time we go to bed. We never get those evil thoughts out of our hearts, yet we wonder how we get so deep into certain sins.

God Wants to Give You a New Heart

> Also, I will give you a new heart, and a new spirit I will put within you. And I will take away the stony heart out of your flesh, and I will give you a heart of flesh.
>
> —Ezekiel 36:26

God will give you a new heart. It doesn't matter what was in your heart before you came to Christ; God will give you a new heart. If you've been struggling in any area we've discussed so far, know that God wants to give you a new heart that is free from the bondage of perversion.

The Bible says, "If any man is in Christ, he is a new creature. Old things have passed away. Look, all things have become new"

(2 Cor. 5:17). God will give you a heart transplant. He will do a miracle in your heart. This is God's promise through the new covenant. It started with the people of Israel. God told them, "I'm going to do something inside of you." Even though it is being taught that once you are a homosexual, you will always be a homosexual, God can still completely transform you. The same is taught about alcoholism: if you were once an alcoholic, you will always be an alcoholic. The devil is a liar. I don't care how much of an alcoholic you were; you can be delivered. And when you are delivered, you are no longer an alcoholic. You are a new creature in Christ. When God delivers you from alcoholism, you can't even stand the taste of it anymore. When God delivers you from smoking, you don't even like the way cigarettes smell anymore. You wonder how you ever smoked.

When God changes your heart, you are no longer the same person you were before. There may be temptations that try to pull you back into your previous lifestyle, but you can shut those down. You don't have to be a homosexual or a lesbian anymore; you don't have to be a fornicator or adulterer. God is saying, "When I do this work in your heart, there is going to be such a miracle that people are going to say they can't believe it. They will wonder how you left that lifestyle." The kind of change I am speaking of has to be an inside job.

We have testimonies of transgendered people who have gotten saved. Some even had sex changes. We tend to think that if someone goes that far, they are reprobate. But nothing is too far for God's reach. God can do a miracle in the person's life and change his or her heart. There is nothing impossible with God. All things are possible to him who believes. Do you believe that?

CHAPTER 6

PRIDE: THE SPIRITUAL BLOCKER

Pride goes before destruction, and a haughty spirit before a fall.

—PROVERBS 16:18

WE'VE BEEN GOING strong in identifying the cluster of demons that ravish the life of a person who has been deeply affected by all kinds of rejection. I pray that while you are reading this book, your expectation is building for a great turnaround—a reversal—in your life and the lives of those for whom you are praying and believing. As we enter this chapter on pride, I want to remind you that there is nothing too hard for God. Though pride is a stubborn demon that shows up in almost every known demonic cluster, God is more stubborn still—stubborn enough to rescue you.

In Job 41 pride manifests itself in the spirit realm as Leviathan, the crooked sea serpent. Spirits operating within the demonic cluster of pride include arrogance, haughtiness, puffed up, self-exaltation, vanity, rebellion, stubbornness, scorning, defiance, anti-submissiveness, egotism, perfection, and the spirits of Rahab and Orion.

Pride brings destruction and a curse, causing a person to err (Ps. 119:21). God resists the proud (James 4:6). The fear of the Lord is to hate pride and arrogance (Prov. 8:13). God attempts to hide pride from man through dreams (Job 33:14–17). Sometimes sickness is the result of pride (Job 33:19–26). God is able to abase those who walk in pride (Dan. 4:37). This spirit blocks prayer, worship, and the moving of the Holy Spirit.

Within the rejection personality the spirit of pride convinces a person, "You really do have a lot to be proud of." This cluster of demons even helps "promote self-advertising publicity campaigns to convince others" and forces "the gauge of inferiorities and low self-image to rise to an unreasonable level, and covers over the warning of Proverbs 27:2—'Let another praise you, and not your own mouth; someone else, and not your own lips.'"[1]

KING OF PRIDE—LEVIATHAN

> Canst thou draw out leviathan with an hook? or his tongue with a cord which thou lettest down?...He beholdeth all high things: he is a king over all the children of pride.
>
> —JOB 41:1, 34, KJV

In the last chapter I introduced the concept of demonic kingdoms. Pride is another demonic kingdom that establishes occupancy in the soul of a person who is oppressed with a spirit of rejection. In this kingdom the demon-king is Leviathan.

> Job 41 is the key passage on leviathan. Most of the people who have this powerful spirit never get deliverance because one of his chief jobs is to block deliverance. Ministers who refuse to open up to the ministry of deliverance are being controlled by a leviathan spirit. This is their chief problem. Most of the people who fight the deliverance ministry have powerful leviathan demons, and are therefore rarely delivered.[2]

Those involved in the deliverance ministry will be familiar with Leviathan. But if you aren't, you may be surprised when you encounter spirits that identify themselves as Leviathan. Some Bible translations refer to him as "the crocodile" or a large sea serpent. Job 41 is the key passage on Leviathan. I talk about this demonic kingdom in depth in my book *Spiritual Warfare and Deliverance Manual*, but I will briefly describe its characteristics again here as we develop a spiritual strategy specifically focused on destroying the spirit of rejection.

Unable to flow in the Holy Spirit

> His scales are his pride, shut up tightly as with a seal. One is so near to another that no air can come between them.
>
> —Job 41:15–16

Leviathan's scales are his pride, and as the verse says, no air can come between them. Air represents spirit, and one of the manifestations of pride is the inability to flow in the Spirit.

Leviathan will attempt to block the flow and manifestations of the Holy Spirit in the assembly of believers. Proud people can hinder the flow of the Spirit; humility is a key to operating in the power of the Holy Spirit.

Self-preserving

Leviathan's scales are his pride. He protects himself with armor. Proud people have a way of closing themselves off and hiding behind the scales of pride. When attacking Leviathan, we attack and strip his scales.

Blocks prayer and prayer ministry

> Will he make many supplications unto thee?
>
> —Job 41:3, KJV

Supplication is prayer, and Leviathan does not make supplication because he is too proud. Leviathan will therefore attempt to block prayer and attack prayer ministries. We have dealt with people who get sleepy when praying and found that it can be connected to Leviathan.

When we pray, we should always approach God with a spirit of humility. The concept of supplication in Bible verses such as Philippians 4:6 is about submitting a request to one who is in authority over us. God is our creator, our ruler. He is sovereign. He is to be reverenced and feared. He is our ultimate help. But those who operate with a spirit of pride will have the attitude that they don't even need God, that they don't need His covering and protection. Pride will cause us to strive and work things out on our own. Pride causes us to lean to our own understanding, which is, at the very least, limited. We cut God's infinite wisdom and unlimited strength and provision out of the picture, and we set ourselves up for failure and burnout, among other things.

Speaks harsh words

> Will he speak soft words unto thee?
>
> —Job 41:3, kjv

Leviathan does not speak soft words. Harsh words are another sign of Leviathan. He speaks roughly, without tenderness or kindness.

Job 41:21 says, "His breath kindles coals," meaning that his words have a destructive, negative effect. Those under Leviathan's power become very critical, especially of those in authority. They become judgmental, and their words have the effect of pulling down rather than building up.

Pride is a mean spirit. People who are prideful disregard the feelings and needs of others. There is no consideration in the way that they interact with other people. They speak to them however they want. But this is not how we as believers are to carry on in our day-to-day conversation with others. We should always be walking in love, grace, humility, and kindness.

Breaks covenant

> Will he make a covenant with thee?
>
> —JOB 41:4, KJV

Leviathan does not keep covenant. He is a covenant-breaking spirit. Many marriages have suffered because of the operation of Leviathan. A marriage will not survive if the spouses are prideful and lack the desire to submit to one another. Look at what Pastor Ron Phillips says about Leviathan:

> When someone is affected by this spirit, it destroys covenant relationships. This spirit breaks up marriages, business partnerships, friendships, and, worst of all, churches.[3]

Pride makes you think you don't need anyone, that you can do everything on your own. It leads you to see people as resources to leverage and use to achieve your own ends. Pride keeps you from experiencing the intimacy of relationship, collaboration, and exchanging thought and ideas. It keeps you from seeing the value in others. Pride will lead you to compete rather than collaborate. You will have a "me vs. the world" mentality.

For prideful people, honoring covenant is not possible. They do not see the blessings of walking in covenant. With covenant, you have to be willing to compromise, to give and take, to hear and sometimes act on behalf of another. Leviathan hardens the hearts of those he possesses, causing them to reject covenant—even covenant with God. People controlled by Leviathan do not value others; therefore they cannot honor others by keeping their word to them. Marriages, friendships, and families are the types of covenantal relationships that fall apart because one party is subject to pride.

Hates serving but likes to be served

> Wilt thou take him for a servant for ever?
>
> —Job 41:4, KJV

Leviathan does not serve. Pride will prevent us from serving one another. Serving is an act of humility, and Leviathan hates it.

Prideful people do not have the capacity to serve others. Service requires humility. As the Bible points out, pride is the same as the spirit of haughtiness. Haughtiness means that you are convinced that you are better than those around you, entitled to esteem, honor, and a higher station. Controlled by this spirit, you will feel that you need to be served, that you deserve to be served.

Not to be played with

> Wilt thou play with him as with a bird? or wilt thou bind him for thy maidens?
>
> —Job 41:5, KJV

Don't play with pride. He is not a pet. It would be dangerous to attempt to do so. This spirit cannot be tamed and therefore has to be renounced completely.

Difficult to defeat

> Lay thine hand upon him, remember the battle, do no more.
>
> —Job 41:8, KJV

The battle with pride may be one of the most difficult battles you will encounter. Pride is very strong in the lives of many, and it will take a fierce determination to defeat it. Even when you are dealing with another person who is full of pride, you may feel as if you are in a battle.

Stiff-necked and stubborn

> In his neck remaineth strength.
>
> —JOB 41:22, KJV

Leviathan is stiff-necked. Stubbornness and rebellion are signs of Leviathan. Israel was always called a stiff-necked people, and God judged them for their stubbornness and rebellion.

> Rebellion is as the sin of witchcraft, and stubbornness is as iniquity and idolatry.
>
> —1 SAMUEL 15:23

> You stiff-necked people, uncircumcised in heart and ears! You always resist the Holy Spirit. As your fathers did, so do you.
>
> —ACTS 7:51

Hard of heart

> His heart is as firm as a stone; yea, as hard as a piece of the nether millstone.
>
> —JOB 41:24, KJV

Hardness of heart is another characteristic of Leviathan. It is also a root cause of divorce (Matt. 19). Hardness of heart is connected to unbelief and the inability to understand and comprehend spiritual things.

Deeply rooted

> He maketh the deep to boil like a pot: he maketh the sea like a pot of ointment.
>
> —Job 41:31, kjv

Leviathan dwells in the deep. Pride can become deeply rooted in our lives and can be difficult to pull out. Leviathan is in the sea, which represents the nations. He causes the deep to boil and is responsible for restlessness.

Controlling and resists submission

Apostle Colin Urquhart has studied the spirit of Leviathan and says that because of its pride, Leviathan wants to be in control. And those under the influence of this spirit "want to control situations in which they are placed. They resist submission to true spiritual authority." He says that Leviathan is "a mocking spirit, and uses mockery as one way of attacking others. It will mock those who [are] walking in obedience to the Lord or who disagree with them, so important to them are their own opinions." Urquhart points out that people with a strong spirit of pride not only become hard-hearted, but they also become thick-skinned. This points back to the tight scales of this reptile-like spirit that function like armor. "The truth bounces off them!" he says.[4]

Deceptive

Leviathan twists the truth. It misrepresents what has been said, causing people to sometimes believe the very opposite of what was said. Those under its influence hear things in a twisted way, and then they pass on this twisted version, often believing it to be the truth. It is this twisting of the truth that makes it a difficult spirit to deal with.

You cannot reason with this spirit because it blinds people to the truth. In fact, those under its influence can be so deceived that they do not appreciate that they are deceived or are twisting the truth.

Isaiah 27:1 says, "In that day the LORD with His fierce and great and strong sword will punish Leviathan the fleeing serpent, even Leviathan the twisted serpent."

> Here is how this deceiving spirit operates. Something is said from the Word and before you hear it, he twists it! You hear it wrong. Maybe you speak to your mate about an issue meaning good—but he or she is angered by it. Some decision is made in church and "it is what it is"; yet you feel there must be more. Or someone infected with Leviathan twists what has been said and creates division.... This serpent gets between you and me and twists the truth. He gets between friends and marital partners and twists. He gets into church life and twists.... In an instant the crocodile takes its prey and twists it around until it takes the life out of it.... The enemy will take good people and twist them until confusion comes.[5]

DEFEAT LEVIATHAN WITH THE POWER OF GOD AND FASTING

> You crushed the heads of Leviathan in pieces, and gave him for food to the people inhabiting the wilderness.
>
> —PSALM 74:14

God has the power to smite and break Leviathan's head, which represents its authority. God is our king, who is working salvation (deliverance) in the earth.

The psalmist said, "I humbled my soul with fasting" (Ps. 35:13). He knew that humility is a great weapon against pride, and it also invites the grace of God (James 4:6) into the battle to give another level of strength against this stubborn demon. When we fast, we humble our souls. Deliverance from Leviathan brings peace, favor, joy, and liberty.

Pharaoh was a Leviathan. God released his people from Pharaoh's grip through terrible judgments. The people of Israel left Egypt and journeyed to the Promised Land, a land flowing with milk and honey. Prosperity will come with deliverance from Leviathan.

The Leviathan spirit can only be overcome through the supernatural activity of God's Spirit, not by any human means. This spirit produces a hardness of heart in people (Job 41:24), making it even more difficult to bring those being used by this spirit to the repentance they need.

As you begin to throw off and dismantle spirits that operate within the spirit of rejection, know that your bout with pride will be the toughest of them all. It is at the root of our fallen nature. It goes deep into the spirit of man. But you can win, though not without humbling yourself before God and seeking Him for deliverance. You will not win against Leviathan in your own strength.

CHAPTER 7

THE SPIRIT OF INFIRMITY

A merry heart does good like a medicine, but a broken spirit dries the bones.

—PROVERBS 17:22

PASTOR CHRIS SIMPSON of New Wine Media teaches on the effects that rejection can have on a person's physical health. He says:

> Did you know that rejection can affect you physically? It can dry up your bones. Generally, it's the "internalizers" that tend to get sick from their rejection. Why is that? It's because rejection often produces anger. And you have to do something with your anger. If you bury it inside, it'll find a way to the surface. If you live in denial concerning your anger, then you'll be resentful and bitter. These attitudes can bring physical problems.
>
> I've often seen people healed on the spot when they forgave those that had hurt them, and when they renounced the bitterness and resentment in their heart. It's amazing how quickly the Holy Spirit will heal and bring life to the dried bones. Many sicknesses and physical maladies tend to be rooted in rejection and bitterness: skin problems, headaches, allergies, neck or back aches, stiffness of joints, arthritis, pains, stress, nervousness, and various diseases.[1]

Though I covered this discussion in my book *Unshakeable,* I believe that the link between rejection and the spirit of infirmity is too important not to include here again. Certain illnesses and disorders have direct links to various manifestations of rejection, whether it be self-rejection, fear, shame, bitterness, resentment, perversion, or unforgiveness. How you receive spiritual healing in your body is related to how you've dealt with rejection.

Even though I am approaching this topic from a spiritual perspective, I want to make it clear that illness is not always demonic. Germs, viruses, and bacteria have legitimate physical impact on our bodies. But we need to be able to discern when an illness is a spiritual attack. There comes a point when we cannot ignore the spiritual roots to some of our physical ailments. When our sickness is strictly physical, physical treatments bring healing and relief. When our sicknesses are spiritual in nature, only deliverance will bring complete healing.

I want to make sure I draw a clear distinction between physical illness and illness brought on by spiritual oppression. For example, you may know someone who is always sick. They are always sneezing, coughing, wheezing, and going to the doctor for antibiotics. It is likely that they have a weakened immune system. It could be viral or bacterial—something that is medically diagnosed. But why has their immune system become so compromised? Why are they not able to fight off infections, germs, or viruses like other people? As I will show in this chapter, self-rejection, guilt, and unforgiveness are common spiritual problems that keep people tormented with sickness and disease. Even the medical community is discovering the correlation.

Neither science nor medicine is our enemy. There are doctors who have wisdom and a gift to help and heal. But there are some things they just can't treat. And when you have been plagued with illness, you are not just interested in treating the symptoms.

Much of what is called medicine today is simply about prescribing drugs that don't get to the root problem. They just minimize the symptoms. Doctors are not trained to diagnose illnesses with deep spiritual roots. But we know who is, and He has given us the blessing of deliverance ministry to heal us mind, body, and spirit.

He Carried Our Sickness and Disease

> He was despised and rejected of men, a man of sorrows and acquainted with grief. And we hid, as it were, our faces from him; he was despised, and we did not esteem him. Surely *he has borne our grief and carried our sorrows*; yet we esteemed him stricken, smitten of God, and afflicted. But he was wounded for our transgressions, he was bruised for our iniquities; the chastisement of our peace was upon him, and by his stripes we are healed.
>
> —Isaiah 53:3–5, emphasis added

Through an in-depth study of Matthew 8:17, which references the above passage, I have come to understand that *griefs* and *sorrows* in this verse literally mean "sickness" and "disease." Matthew quotes the prophet Isaiah, saying, "When the evening came, they brought to Him many who were possessed with demons. And He cast out the spirits with His word, and healed all who were sick, to fulfill what was spoken by Isaiah the prophet, 'He Himself took our infirmities and bore our sicknesses'" (vv. 16–17).

According to these verses, Isaiah's prophecy of Jesus's bearing of our griefs and carrying our sorrows was fulfilled by His casting out demons and healing the sick. The prophet is on to something, as sickness and infirmity do cause grief and sorrow.

As I will point out later, one of the main strategies for destroying the spirit of rejection is the revelation of Christ's rejection. Isaiah brings it up in Isaiah 53:3–5, as there is a connection between Jesus's rejection and His carrying of our griefs and sorrows (sicknesses and infirmities). We will find rejection at the root of most of the sorrow and grief we experience. Rejection is also the root cause of much sickness and infirmity. Rejection is one of the worse things the enemy can cause to happen in a person's life. It opens him or her up to so much.

Authors and deliverance pioneers Noel and Phyl Gibson wrote a book many years ago that I believe is one of the best resources on the spirit of rejection. It is called *Excuse Me, Your Rejection Is Showing.* In the book they refer to rejection as the masterpiece of Satan. He uses rejection to try to destroy everyone who comes into the world. Rejection functions as a doorkeeper (usher) to the demonic world. It is a root problem, a root demon. As I have already stated, when it comes to deliverance, you have to get to the root. The axe is laid to the root (Matt. 3:10; Luke 3:9). You can break branches off. You can break symptoms off. But unless you go to the root and pull it up from there, it grows back like a weed.

Deliverance Gets to the Root of Disease

Medical doctors primarily deal with empirical evidence—what they see on charts and tests. They don't often prescribe treatment based on whether or not a person is dealing with rejection, anger, or bitterness. Psychiatrists may get into some of the psychological issues of why a person is suffering with a disease or illness, but if they are not believers, they won't seek to access the spiritual state of a person. But deliverance is a ministry that is designed to get to root problems. The problem with roots is that you can't see them with the natural eye. They are often hidden underground, only to be discerned by the Spirit of God.

Many medical professionals are just now beginning to accept that there is such a strong link between the health of our spirits and the health of our bodies and minds. The Bible says in 3 John 2, "Beloved, I pray that all may go well with you and that you may be in good health, even as your soul is well."

Unless you understand deliverance and the spirit realm, you won't be able to diagnose what you or the people around you are dealing with. You may think that you have to accept just trying to get over your sickness by faith. Then if you remain ill, you may feel condemnation because you believe that your lack of faith is keeping you sick. There are some cases where a person's level of faith plays a major part of their deliverance and healing. But you need a full understanding of God's deliverance to deal with the root problem, which is demons.

The Bible doesn't use our modern terminology to name every sickness and disease. It does tell us that by casting out demons with His word and healing all those who were sick, Jesus took their sicknesses and infirmities—He lifted them off of the people (Matt. 8:16). When we hear sermons and messages that God is our healer, Matthew 8:17 is what many pastors focus on: "He Himself took our infirmities and bore our sicknesses." And with a Word of Faith–type understanding, we are encouraged to confess our healing by faith. What happens is that we don't look at verse 17 in the context of verse 16: "...they brought to Him many who were possessed with demons. And He cast out the spirits with His word, and healed all who were sick..." Then verse 17 continues, "...to fulfill..." Many times we separate these two verses, but really, healing from sickness and infirmity often comes through casting out demons.

There's an old debate that pops up every so often about whether or not Christians can have demons. The answer is yes, they can. A person is made up of three parts—spirit, soul, and body. The Holy Spirit dwells in the spirit part of man. Demons take up residence in the soul. The soul contains the mind, will, and emotions. Demons' occupancy in this area of a person is why the Bible says that our minds have to be renewed.

To further prove that Christians can't have demons, some people may argue that God can't take up residence in a place that is also occupied by the devil. Obviously this is not true. Since God is omnipresent (everwhere at the same time), which means He is in heaven but also on the earth, and demons are roaming the earth, God and the demons are essentially occupying the same space. So that myth has been disproven, showing Christians can have demons and need deliverance from them.

You Don't Have to Be Tormented

> Then his master, after he had summoned him, said to him, "O you wicked servant! I forgave you all that debt because you pleaded with me. Should you not also have had compassion on your fellow servant, even as I had pity on you?" His master was angry and delivered him to the jailers until he should pay all his debt. So also My heavenly Father will do to each of you, if from your heart you do not forgive your brother for his trespasses.
>
> —Matthew 18:32–35

This is the story of a man who had been forgiven much, but he did not extend forgiveness to his fellow servant, so the man was handed over to tormentors. Tormentors represent demons. In centuries past, when a person was in debt, he could be jailed and then turned over to the tormentors (people hired to torture, harass, and humiliate them during their prison term). Though we don't have debtor's prisons today, we can be sued or our wages garnished for certain unpaid debts. We definitely don't want to live our lives being tormented by the enemy. So we often need healing from the root of bitterness that stems from being rejected and that keeps us from extending forgiveness. This forgiveness is the gift of God.

But because many people will not forgive, they have been turned over to the tormentors of sickness and disease.

BITTERNESS AND UNFORGIVENESS ARE KILLING YOU

The connection between rejection, rebellion, and bitterness to physical and psychological illness is not new in deliverance ministry. In the medical field it is becoming more and more recognized as a legitimate link. But what is good is that for those who need it, there is a growing library of research proving the connection between rejection and physical diseases and illnesses.

Rejection, bitterness, resentment, and unforgiveness open the door for arthritis, cancer, autoimmune disorders, and many other ailments. But in my almost forty years in deliverance ministry, two of the main health problems I've recognized in people who are bitter are cancer and arthritis. I am not saying that everyone who has these diseases is dealing with bitterness, rejection, or any other demons. I am saying that these spiritual issues *could be* a root cause. The Spirit of God has revealed to us such connections, and we have seen people healed from these diseases during deliverance ministry.

Another interesting thing is that the older we get, the more likely it will be that our bodies begin to tire under the weight of things like bitterness and anger; we begin to develop some of these illnesses later in life. Sometimes we wave them off as diseases that just come with old age, but in fact it is prolonged bitterness that causes these health issues.

Anger and rage, both rooted in bitterness, have pronounced effects on the autonomic nervous system and the immune system. Your immune system, of course, is what protects you from disease and sickness. When your immune system is not working properly, you have increased chances to get sick. When you are full of anger, rage, or fear, the adrenaline level in your blood is increased, which gets your body ready to fight or run. This is known as the fight-or-flight syndrome. In this state your immune response is low. If this reaction remains engaged over long periods of time, you can become ill. Being wound up with anger, fear, and even stress is a normal everyday occurrence for many people in society, yet this is a destructive place to be.

You've probably heard a lot being said about autoimmune disease or disorders. Bitterness, unforgiveness, and self-rejection are the spiritual roots behind these diseases. Autoimmune responses occur when you become allergic to certain parts of your own body. This is when your own body turns on itself and attacks itself with diseases such as arthritis, fibromyalgia, lupus, certain heart issues, some cancers, type 1 diabetes, and various allergies. These are what were previously called "collagen diseases," but are now called autoimmune diseases.

The root of bitterness stems from repressed anger and rage, and there is usually a root of unforgiveness, which can be pointed toward yourself, others, or God. This means that any area in your body is a potential target for the enemy. In the chart titled "Spirit of Rejection Meets Spirit of Infirmity" I have listed some physical conditions that coulbe be a result of bitterness and unforgiveness as well as other demons found in the rejection, rebellion, and bitterness clusters.[2]

You will see many of the issues repeat themselves. The devil comes to steal, kill, and destroy. He knows what will destroy a person. Rejection opens the door to all the spiritual roots that you see here. I have categorized the various infirmities by common issues that occur in the body. The list is not exhaustive, and I am not attempting to give medical advice or diagnoses. This information is for you to take before the Lord and seek the guidance of the Holy Spirit concerning how your or a loved one's body may be affected by spirits that operate within the rejection family of demons. And remember, just because you have been diagnosed or suffer from any of these illnesses does not mean they automatically have a spiritual root. This is why discernment is key.

SPIRIT OF REJECTION MEETS SPIRIT OF INFIRMITY	
INFIRMITIES	**SPIRITUAL ROOTS**
HEART ISSUES	
Heart attack, heart blockage, irregular heartbeat, pain in the chest, breastbone pain, cardiac arrest	Fear, doubt
Aneurysms and strokes, ruptured blood vessels	Rage, anger, hostility, self-rejection, bitterness
Angina, high blood pressure	Fear, stress, anxiety, paranoia, anger

SPIRIT OF REJECTION MEETS SPIRIT OF INFIRMITY	
INFIRMITIES	SPIRITUAL ROOTS
HEART ISSUES (CONT.)	
Cholesterol problems	Anger, paranoia, fear; withholding, inadequacy, insignificance, sorrow, anger, self-deprecation, constantly putting down oneself
Congestive heart failure	Fear, anxiety, bitterness, self-rejection (Luke 21:26)
DIGESTIVE ISSUES	
Anorexia, bulimia, gluttony, weight issues; binge eating, secret abnormal eating, compulsive eating, nonspiritual fasting, and purging	Self-hatred, self-rejection, self-bitterness, lack of self-esteem, insecurity, addiction, compulsive behavior, self-pity, idleness, self-reward, fear of disapproval, rejection, perceived lack of love, frustration, nervousness, resentment, pride; control, witchcraft, self-mutilation, bitterness
Crohn's disease, ulcerative colitis, acid reflux, mucous colitis, spastic colon	Fear, abandonment, rejection, self-rejection, self-bitterness, self-hatred
Colon cancer	Bitterness, slander with the tongue
Ulcers	Fear, stress, anxiety
IMMUNE AND AUTOIMMUNE DISORDERS	
Type 1 diabetes, multiple sclerosis, rheumatoid arthritis, lupus, fibromyalgia, Crohn's disease, thyroid disorders, and other white blood cell deviant behaviors[3]	Self-hatred, self-guilt, self-conflict, self-rejection, self-bitterness, self-conflict[4]
Diabetes	Dissatisfaction, anger, rejection, self-hatred, abuse, abandonment, guilt, criticism, discontented spirit; rejection from a father, husband, or a man

SPIRIT OF REJECTION MEETS SPIRIT OF INFIRMITY	
INFIRMITIES	**SPIRITUAL ROOTS**
IMMUNE AND AUTOIMMUNE DISORDERS (CONT.)	
Colds, flu, virus	Stress, brokenheartedness, self-doubt, guilt
Leukemia	Deep-rooted bitterness, resentment, self-hatred coming from rejection by a father[5]
Allergies	Fear, lack of forgiveness, feelings of inadequacy, insignificance, sorrow, anxiety, stress
SKIN ISSUES	
Acne, rashes, boils, eczema, shingles, and psoriasis	Fear, anxiety
MUSCULAR ISSUES	
Muscle tension, spasms, or pain	Fear, anxiety, stress
BRAIN, NERVE, OR SENSORY DISORDERS	
Ear issues, such as ringing in the ears	Witchcraft, the occult
Multiple sclerosis	Deep self-hatred, shame, self-bitterness, self-rejection
Eye problems	Grief (Ps. 6:7; 31:9)
REPRODUCTIVE ISSUES	
Breast, ovarian, prostate, or uterine cancers	Anger, guilt, self-hatred, self-bitterness; the need to be loved; rejection; promiscuity; uncleanness; self-conflict; self-rejection; self-hatred[6]
BONE DISEASES AND DISORDERS	
Osteoporosis	Bitterness, envy, jealousy (Prov. 12:4; 14:30)[7]
Rheumatoid arthritis	Bitterness, unforgiveness, self-rejection, self-hate, guilt;[8] stress; self-unforgiveness; self-fear; doesn't want to face self-conflict

REVELATION OF HEALING AT MARAH

God is a physician. He wants to puts you back together again so that you can have life and have it more abundantly. Living life broken down by rejection is not what He wants for you. He doesn't want to you have to carry all your hurts throughout life. He wants to sweeten the bitter places in your life just as He did for the people of Israel at Marah:

> When they came to Marah, they could not drink of the waters of Marah, for they were bitter. Therefore, the name of it was called Marah. So the people murmured against Moses, saying, "What shall we drink?"
>
> And he cried to the LORD, and the LORD showed him a tree. When he had thrown it into the waters, the waters were made sweet.
>
> There He made for them a statute and an ordinance, and there He tested them. He said, "If you diligently listen to the voice of the LORD your God, and do what is right in His sight, and give ear to His commandments, and keep all His statutes, I will not afflict you with any of the diseases with which I have afflicted the Egyptians. For I am the LORD who heals you."
>
> —EXODUS 15:23–26

This is the place where God first reveals Himself to His people as Jehovah Rapha, the Lord our Healer. This is the place where the Lord also draws the parallel between bitterness and healing. The name *Marah* means "bitter" and refers to the bitter spring or pool of water that the people of Israel encountered after their exodus from Egypt.[9]

The word *marah*, used throughout the Old Testament, means "bitter, change, be disobedient, disobey, grievously, provocation, provoking." Going further, it is used in a causative connotation:

to make bitter, to cause to rebel, to provoke. Then figuratively it means to resist, to rebel.[10]

In order to heal the waters of Marah, God instructed Moses to throw a tree into the waters, and the waters were made sweet (Exod. 15:23–25). The tree represents Jesus Christ and His cross. Two of the redemptive things Jesus suffered on the cross were being bruised and rejected. Part of His suffering for us was being rejected by men, rejected by His own nation Israel. He was despised and not esteemed. So part of the redemption that Christ came to bring, part of His suffering, was rejection from His own people. Christ had to encounter all that we encounter so that in Him our salvation would be full and complete. The Bible is not shortchanging us when it says that Christ is acquainted with our griefs and sorrows. If anyone knows and cares, Jesus does.

So whatever you are dealing with in life—whether it's rejection, hurt, or bitterness—you can be healed, restored, and made whole. The redemption accomplished at the Cross sweetens the waters. The tree in the form of a cross upon which Christ was hung sweetens the life of every person who accepts His sacrifice. Through salvation—which includes deliverance from bitterness, anger, resentment, rejection, pride, and rebellion—life becomes sweet.

That's what deliverance is all about. Deliverance is salvation. Deliverance is healing. Deliverance is restoration. God wants you whole. God doesn't want you living life messed up. Jesus saves, heals, delivers, restores, and makes whole.

You definitely do not want to grow old being sick, bitter, and mean. People wonder why it seems that some older people are so mean. It's just a manifestation of bitterness. All the years of their lives they have not released any of the hardship they've been through, so by the time they are a certain age, they are mean and grouchy. We can sometimes think that this is just a part of getting old. No, it is not. Those are just old demons.

You do not have to be old and bitter, mean, sick, and all messed up. If you get old and feel you have a right to hate everybody, then the devil has a right to destroy your life. This is not the way God wants His people to live. Deliverance is here. Today is the day of salvation. You can be set free to be full of joy and love even in old age.

So then, it is no wonder that God, in His great love for us all, reveals Himself to the people of Israel as their healer at the bitter waters of Marah. Bitterness and healing go hand in hand. Israel had just come out of Egypt, out of four hundred years of bondage. When you've been in bondage that long, there's a great chance that you will harbor unforgiveness and bitterness toward the people who put you in bondage. But God will bear your bitterness and give you something sweet in exchange—joy for sorrow, beauty for ashes.

Forgive by Faith

There are some hurts, some situations in life, that are not easy to forgive, let go of, and move on from. But this is exactly what you have to do in order to break rejection's destructive cycle in your life. When you stubbornly refuse to let someone go, you refuse to release him and forgive him, saying, "I'll never forgive that person. I will always hate him. I'll not release it. I'll not let it go. You don't know what happened to me. You don't know what he did to me. I have a right to hold on to this. I have a right to be angry. I have a right to be upset with this individual. I will not forgive him." This means you are choosing to stubbornly hold on to unforgiveness. The Bible says, "Stubbornness is as iniquity and idolatry" (1 Sam. 15:23). God's command is to forgive.

You may think that you can't forgive because you don't feel like it. The truth is, there are a lot of things you have to do by faith. You can't go by how you feel because you may feel like punching someone in the face. For you, forgiveness will not only be an act of faith; it will also need to be an act of your will. You may find yourself having to act and say that you forgive them, and then—with God's strength—actually do it. Forgiveness and setting people free will bring healing to your spirit, soul, and body.

Release Guilt and Shame

Guilt is the root of countless diseases and unhappiness. You may have noticed that it showed up more than once in the "Spirit of Rejection Meets Spirit of Infirmity" chart. Guilt is one of the worst things you can allow to control your life. It comes from condemnation, shame, unworthiness, embarrassment, low self-esteem, and feelings of inferiority (low class, bottom of the barrel, always last place, insecure, never good enough). There are people who live their lives feeling guilty about things they did years ago. They have never forgiven themselves for something they did or did not do. They literally punish themselves. They feel unworthy, ashamed, and embarrassed, which often turns into self-rejection.

Guilt is a terrible demon. If you know you harbor feelings of guilt, shame, regret, or worthlessness, you need to get delivered. Ask God to forgive you, and ask the people you may have hurt to forgive you. But the most important thing you need to do to experience complete victory in this area is to forgive yourself. This is the hardest part for many people. They believe God forgives them and other people forgive them, but they can't forgive themselves. This is the point where you take on the righteousness of Christ by faith and by a decision first, confessing it daily if you have to, until it you truly accept it.

Let Jesus Cover You

We have all done things that we are not proud of, but we must remember that when we've done all we can to make things right, Jesus is our righteousness. He covers us. If we don't get this into our spirits, then we are open to being afflicted by many of the physical health issues I have listed. As we've discussed, there is a close connection between the spirit, soul, and body. The Bible says, "I pray that you may prosper in all things and be in health, just as your soul prospers" (3 John 2, NKJV). Your soul is your mind, will, and emotions. If your soul is not healthy and you are overcome with hurt, shame, guilt, fear, and rejection, your body will eventually be affected. It doesn't always happen overnight. The longer you carry these things, the more damage they do.

This is why many of these diseases manifest at an older age. Sometimes younger bodies can resist some of the spiritual trauma better than older bodies that have carried the issues longer. I personally don't believe that as you get older you have to become sickly. I don't believe God designed our bodies to break down. I don't believe He created us to suffer through our senior years. But I do believe that many people are sick in their old age because they have shouldered guilt, resentment, anger, and other negative spirits year after year until their bodies begin to manifest these spirits physically.

Self-rejection, self-pity, self-bitterness, and self-hatred also showed up often in the list of spiritual roots above. Some people think these spirits aren't as bad as a demon like lust. But the thing is, they can do just as much damage to your life as lust. Self-rejection, self-pity, and self-hatred may not always manifest as moral sins such as lust, fornication, adultery, or homosexuality. We tend to see moral demons as the worst kind. When people confess that they are struggling with these self-directed issues, we just pat the person on the back and tell them, "Just hang in there. Everything will be all right." We pet those demons, but these are the kind that cause individuals to destroy themselves. We need to take them seriously and be set free.

For some issues such as cancer, arthritis, type 1 diabetes, and certain heart conditions, we find that the body is attacking itself, and we have uncovered spiritual reasons why it would do this. Obviously I don't know all the ramifications of sickness and disease. I am not claiming any medical expertise, but what I am pointing out is the very real connection between our spiritual condition and our health.

There is still a lot that even doctors are learning concerning this connection. There are many illnesses, such as autoimmune disease, that are hard to find the physical cause for. Sometimes people go their whole lives with no diagnosis. What doctors and scientific researchers are discovering is the link between the spirit, mind, and body in many of these cases. Common issues such as repressed anger, unforgiveness, resentment, bitterness, guilt, shame, fear, insecurity, trauma, abuse, and identity issues are being listed as causal factors in many diseases that doctors had in the past found difficult to diagnose and treat.

Every sickness and disease was not covered in this chapter, but what I hope you are able to get some help with is being able to uncover root issues of bigger health issues more common to us all. God will give you grace to discern specific issues, and He will give you revelation by His Spirit for how to be set free from any demonic spirit that threatens you. Psalm 144:1 says that He prepares our hands for war. In other words, He provides us all that we need to win the battles we face.

[PART II]

DELIVERANCE AND RESTORATION

CHAPTER 8

REJECTION MUST GO!

O God, You have rejected us, You have scattered us; You have been displeased; take us back.

—PSALM 60:1

AS WE'VE DISCOVERED, we have all been rejected in one way or another. In order to stop rejection from destroying our lives, we must be able to identify the causes of rejection and come against the demons of rejection, fear of rejection, self-rejection, hereditary rejection, roots of rejection, and the spirits that come in with rejection: hurt, anger, bitterness, rage, pride, fear, rebellion, and more. All of these things can torment your life. Jesus does not want you to be tormented. He wants you to be set free. You are not alone. So many people need deliverance from these demons of rejection. God wants to set us all free from the spirit of rejection so that we can bring deliverance to our families, friends, and those around us.

Spiritual Truths That Set You Free From Rejection

The Bible says, "If the Son sets you free, you shall be free indeed" (John 8:36). Through Christ we have been set free from every demonic hindrance and attack. The Bible teaches us how to claim freedom from rejection and move into a life of acceptance in the Beloved. Let's look at how we can be set free by the truth in God's Word.

Revealed knowledge

I have already shown how a lack of knowledge leads to destruction. Therefore taking up and seeking after the knowledge of God brings great deliverance. Proverbs says, "Through knowledge the just will be delivered" (Prov. 11:9). The enemy works overtime to keep you from gaining knowledge. He does not want you to learn about deliverance or the demonic realm because he and his demons are creatures of darkness: "For our fight is not against flesh and blood, but against principalities, against powers, against the *rulers of the darkness*" (Eph. 6:12, emphasis added). Satan can only rule where there is darkness or ignorance. So light and revelation expose and weaken his power. You are able to break His power over your life when you know where he is and how he operates.

Churches are not teaching deliverance. There is such a lack of revelation in this area, and people remain bound, groping in darkness. People who are taught and trained in deliverance not only will receive deliverance, but they will also be equipped to minister deliverance. They will become a threat to the kingdom of darkness.

Christ's own rejection

When Jesus came to the earth, He was not received. Even His own people rejected him. Isaiah 53:3 says that He was despised and rejected of men. But He was rejected so that we could be delivered from rejection. He took our rejection upon Himself so that He could deliver us from rejection. Christ experienced every form of rejection possible. He is acquainted with our rejection, with our sorrow and our grief.

The biggest form of rejection came when He said, "My God, My God, why have You forsaken Me?" (Matt. 27:46). It was at that moment He became sin, and He experienced divine rejection. The Father could not accept Him because of all the sins of the world laid upon Him. God always rejects sin. Jesus became sin, went through rejection, suffered, and was beaten, wounded, and bruised in order to deliver us from rejection.

Rejection is a major stronghold, and acceptance in Christ is the central aspect of deliverance and salvation. Because of Christ's rejection we can be accepted in the Beloved. We can be accepted through the blood of Jesus. We can be accepted by grace. We don't have to be perfected through legalism or keeping laws. We can be accepted by faith.

> He chose us in Him before the foundation of the world, that we should be holy and without blame before Him in love, having predestined us to adoption as sons by Jesus Christ to Himself, according to the good pleasure of His will, to the praise of the glory of His grace, by which *He has made us accepted in the Beloved.*
>
> —EPHESIANS 1:4–6, NKJV, EMPHASIS ADDED

This is the tremendous blessing of Christianity. It is the only religion that teaches salvation by grace. Every other religion teaches salvation by works, that somehow you have to earn God's favor. No, our salvation is by grace and faith. Jesus earned it for us, and we can receive it by faith. That is why accepting Christ is the only way to God. It is the only basis of salvation. Every other way is false, is rooted in deception, and opens the door to rejection. People bound by rejection believe they can never measure up to what they are taught about what pleases or appeases God. Rejection always opens the door for you to try to perform your way into being accepted by God, only to be set up for repeating failure.

Religion is what causes people to believe that God is always angry with them, that He is out to punish them for not keeping all of His commandments. Christianity, when practiced in an ungodly form, can be religious in this way. Many individuals have been hurt by churches who operate in a strict, man-made form of godliness. Whenever man tries to interpret what God wants rather than receiving *His* plans and purposes by faith, we get into religion.

Look at the religion of Islam. Muslims have to pray five times a day and go to Mecca at least once in their lifetime. They have to do this and that, always performing, always trying to earn Allah's love. Ishmael is the father of the Arabic people, many of whom are Muslim. Remember, Ishmael was rejected by God as the promised son of Abraham. So a spirit of rejection is in Ishmael's bloodline. That root of rejection has opened up an entire culture to being deceived into thinking they can earn their way into heaven. The good news is that there is deliverance through Jesus Christ.

Look at the Indian caste system. It is loaded with rejection. Hinduism is about being in the right caste—if you're in a low caste, you're rejected. Hindus are taught that if they do what is good in this life, they may be able to come back as something better in the next life. So there is always a performance orientation in their culture. They work at being perfect, and they work at being accepted.

That's what rejected people do: they work and work and work for society, for God, or for others to accept them. The truth is, you can only be accepted by grace, faith, and mercy. You need to get delivered from any spirits that try to make you perform up to the level of society or other people to make you accepted. Now that doesn't mean that you shouldn't do what is right to be accepted; it simply means that the desire to be accepted should not drive you and dominate your life. If it does, then it's demonic.

Warfare prayer

Prayer is a very powerful weapon in the fight against rejection. Prayer brings you into the presence of God. Prayer opens up your spirit to hear the truth of your acceptance through Christ. Prayer builds up your inner man.

Psalm 144:1 is a prayer you should consistently pray over your life, so that you will be able to fight against spiritual opposition that comes against your life. I mentioned this verse at the end of the last chapter. The verse reads in its entirety, "Blessed be the Lord my strength, who prepares my hands for war, and my fingers to fight." Confess, believe, and count on God to give you the strategy to gain victory over rejection.

One of the most inspirational psalms when it comes to spiritual warfare is Psalm 18. Praying some of the key verses in this chapter will build your faith to see great deliverance in your life. For example, verse 19 says that deliverance brings us into a large or broad place.

Many of you have bought books in my Prayers for Spiritual Battle series. The prayers in those books were birthed out of times when the Lord led me to His Word and instructed me to pray psalms such as Psalm 144 and Psalm 18. The Bible is full of passages that build faith, courage, and boldness to trample over all the works of the enemy.

Sometimes the enemy wants to confine, restrict, and limit us. But through spiritual warfare we can break the limitations. We can ask God to deliver us from demons that block and obstruct our way so that we can come into a larger place. Rejection is one of the demons that make it hard for us to move to the next level in our lives. But the Lord has given you the necks of your enemies, and you will destroy them in His name (Ps. 18:40).

Second Samuel 19:3 is another scripture we use during deliverance ministry at our church because sometimes the enemy tries to bring rejection into our lives by stealth, or when we are unaware, and it comes in undetected. A stealth bomber goes under the radar, making it hard for the radar to detect it. The military developed stealth technology to make it easier to enter a region undetected and cause damage. So I encourage people to pray 2 Samuel 19:3 to expose, bind, and cast out the rejection demon that would try by stealth or undetection to come into their lives. This verse works against any demonic spirit that tries to sneak into your life undetected.

The anointing of God

Psalm 18:50 says, "He gives great deliverance to His king, and shows lovingkindness to His anointed." If you are saved and baptized in the Holy Spirit, you are God's anointed. Therefore God wants to give you great deliverance whenever the enemy attacks. You can pray, "God, I am Your anointed, and You give me great deliverance over the spirit of rejection." He will do it; He will show mercy to you and give you victory over it.

Persistence

> I pursued my enemies and overtook them; I did not return until they were destroyed.
>
> —Psalm 18:37

This is persistence. This is being a person who will not be turned back or scared away by the enemy. Persistent individuals do not stop until the enemy has been overtaken and defeated, whether it's witchcraft, sickness, poverty, or rejection. Determine that you will take up a persistent, persevering spirit against the working of the enemy in your life. Whatever is attacking your life, do not retreat until it is completely annihilated by the power of God.

Authority in the Spirit

One of the most important principles of spiritual warfare is that you must use your authority against the enemy. Jesus said, "I give unto *you* power [*power* is the Greek word *exousia*, which means 'authority'] to tread on serpents and scorpions, and over all the power of the enemy: and nothing shall by any means hurt you" (Luke 10:19, KJV, emphasis added). Now some people say you can't be hurt by the enemy because Jesus says, "I give you power." But that's only if you use the authority.

Just because you have been given authority doesn't mean you've used it. If you don't exercise your authority, you cannot claim the second part of that verse that says "nothing shall by any means hurt you." We must exercise our authority, and some of the ways we do that are through prayer, through binding and loosing, and through commands and decrees that we release through our words. So it's important to exercise your authority over the enemy on a consistent basis.

Remember the story of the Gergesene demoniacs in Matthew chapter 8? There were two of them in the account. The Bible says that they blocked the road. Those two demonized men would not let anyone pass that way. It is a picture of how demons will try to block your way. You need to bind and rebuke in the name of Jesus any demon that will try to block your path or your way.

Psalm 91:13 says, "You shall tread upon the lion and adder; the young lion and the serpent you shall trample underfoot." The enemy is under your feet. That represents total authority and victory. Make this your confession, and go forth in victory and in the power of God.

Be Set Free!

God wants to set us free from the spirit of rejection so that we can bring deliverance to our families, friends, and those around us. Jesus said, "The Spirit of the Lord is upon Me, because He has anointed Me to preach the gospel to the poor; He has sent Me to heal the broken-hearted, to preach deliverance to the captives" (Luke 4:18). He imparted this responsibility to us as well.

But you must minister deliverance to yourself first. Jesus talked about this when He said, "First cast out the beam out of thine own eye; and then shalt thou see clearly to cast out the mote out of thy brother's eye" (Matt. 7:5, KJV). That phrase "cast out" carries the same meaning when the Bible speaks, in other passages, of casting out demons. It is the Greek word *ekballō*, which means "to expel or eject."[1]

We must be able to identify the causes of rejection in order to come against the demons of rejection, fear of rejection, self-rejection, hereditary rejection, roots of rejection, and the spirits that come in with rejection: hurt, anger, bitterness, rage, pride, fear, rebellion, and more. All of these things can torment your life. This is not God's plan for you. He wants you to be set free. You are not alone. So many people need deliverance from these demons of rejection and the other demons that accompany them. And sometimes the key to their deliverance is first yours. You can blaze a trail for deliverance, and your testimony will build others' faith for their own deliverance.

CHAPTER 9

REBUILDING THE GATES AND WALLS

Then I became very much afraid and said to the king, "May the king live forever! Why should not my face be troubled when the city, the place of my fathers' tombs, lies waste, and its gates have been destroyed by fire?" So the king said to me, "What are you requesting about this matter?" Immediately, I prayed to the God of heaven and then said to the king, "If this pleases the king and if this might be good for your servant who is before you, then would you send me to Judah, to the city of my fathers' tombs so that I may rebuild it?"

—NEHEMIAH 2:2–5

NEHEMIAH WAS ONE of the captives in Babylon; there he served as a cupbearer to the Babylonian king Artaxerxes. Nehemiah's story takes place seventy years after Jeremiah prophesied Israel's captivity and his lamentations. Israel was about to be released from Babylon by decree of Cyrus, the king of Persia, whom God stirred up to release the people to go back to the land to rebuild Jerusalem and its walls. This return is a picture of our spiritual rebuilding after judgment and after desolation by the attacks of the enemy.

In Nehemiah chapter 1 we learn that Nehemiah received a burden. After hearing about how the people in the land were suffering and about how the land was desolated—the city was burned, and the walls and the gates had been destroyed—he wept and went into fasting and mourning. The king saw his downcast countenance and asked, "What is wrong with you?"

The king was not a Jew; he was a heathen king. But because God rules over all kings, God had already put it in King Artaxerxes's heart to rebuild what had been destroyed in the city. So when Nehemiah told the king what was troubling him—that his city was left in ruin, the gates were burned with fire, the walls were destroyed, and he had no rest knowing the condition of the city that he loved—the king was ready to grant him official permission, including finances and troops, to go back to the land and rebuild the walls. The king even commanded his army to accompany Nehemiah because Babylon was some distance from Jerusalem and there were nations between the two cities that were hostile toward the Jews. These other people did not want to see Jerusalem restored.

One of the first things that you need to understand if you are believing God for restoration in your life is that the enemy will fight to prevent you from being restored. He is not going to make it easy. You have to be determined.

In this chapter I will use the story of Nehemiah as a picture of what it means in the spirit to restore spiritual gates and walls in an individual's life. Physical cities during the time in which Nehemiah lived had physical walls and physical gates to protect them from enemies. At night they would close the gates. They had watchmen on the walls. In the spirit we are like a city that has gates and walls. If our spiritual gates and walls have been destroyed, it means the enemy has access to our lives.

Walls and gates represent protection and entry points into a city. When a person's walls have been destroyed by sin, rebellion, trauma, abuse, hurt, or rejection, they don't have any protection from the enemy; he can come in and wreak havoc in the person's life. The only way you can protect yourself from demonic attack is to make sure your gates and your walls have been restored.

In Nehemiah's day the gates of the city were open during the day and monitored. Watchmen were able to keep tabs on who would come and go. At night the gates were closed so that the enemy of the city could not enter in. So the story of Nehemiah's restoring the walls and gate of Jerusalem is a picture of spiritual warfare. We need our gates and walls—the gates of our minds, our hearts, our emotions, and our souls—to be closed to the enemy. We need our walls built up so the enemy cannot come and go as he pleases.

Like a City Without Walls

Proverbs 25:28 says, "He who has no rule over his own spirit is like a city that is broken down and without walls." This verse is telling us that if you have no control of your temper—you get angry too quickly—or your emotions—you get depressed too quickly—then you don't rule your spirit. You are like a city that is broken down and without walls.

You cannot allow your mind, emotions, or temper to be out of control. If you do, the devil will have access to your life. The Bible says, "Do not let the sun go down on your wrath, nor give place to the devil" (Eph. 4:26–27, NKJV).

In my years of ministry I have seen what happens when people have no self-control. They don't control their tongues, thoughts, tempers, or emotions. They allow themselves to get into depression for weeks at a time. They get angry. They say anything. They do anything. They lose it too quickly. And then the enemy comes in and destroys their life. This happens because they are like an open city with no walls, no restraint.

They have given place to the devil and have become a walking target for his schemes. He can now enter in and destroy and devastate their lives.

Initially the enemy tries to destroy us through trauma, sin, rebellion, rejection, and so on. Deliverance is one of the ways we get restored. Everyone has gone through something in life, and we all need some restoration somewhere—some people more than others. Some people have been molested, raped, physically and verbally abused, hurt, and/or rejected; as a result they are bitter, angry, addicted, and bound. The enemy has tried to destroy their lives. Everyone needs healing and restoration. That's what deliverance is all about.

THE SPIRIT OF SHAME

> They said to me, "The remnant that returned from captivity is there in the province enduring great *affliction and reproach. Also, the wall of Jerusalem remains broken down, and its gates have been burned with fire.*" When I heard these words, I sat down and wept and mourned for days. Then I fasted, and prayed before the God of heaven.
>
> —NEHEMIAH 1:3–4, EMPHASIS ADDED

So here's the picture: The remnant of Israel were greatly afflicted, which means they were tormented, oppressed, and poverty-stricken. Because of their captivity and the broken-down state of Jerusalem they bore heavy reproach, which correlates with shame. The spirit of shame is one of the worst demons that can come into your life. No one likes to be run down and beat up in life. No one likes to be whipped, defeated, afflicted, poor, broken, devastated, and oppressed. It's shameful. It's embarrassing because God did not create us to be shamed.

When you meet a person whose life has been devastated, even though they may not say it, there is a shame that the enemy has put on them. What I hate about the devil is that he destroys your life, and then he tries to make you feel bad about it. He beats you down. He's the instrument. Sometimes it's rebellion, but he's the instrument. Then he tries to beat you down with hopelessness, despair, despondency, discouragement, depression, doubt, and unbelief. You catch yourself thinking or saying things such as: "I'll never get out of this." "This is horrible." "I can't do any better." The devil wants to beat you down.

This was the condition Nehemiah found Jerusalem in. The people of Israel were in reproach, all because of rebellion. But God still had a plan to restore them. He moved upon the hearts of Nehemiah and a heathen king to rebuild Jerusalem's gates and walls. He did this because the whole history of Israel paints a spiritual picture of His plan to save, deliver, and restore all people.

The Bible is not a history book of random events written so that we could read nice Bible stories. It is applicable to our lives. God wants to give you hope and show you that if a natural city can be rebuilt, then your spiritual city can be rebuilt. If the natural city of Jerusalem was messed up, burned up, and then restored, then no matter what your condition is, by the spirit of God your life can also be restored.

Nehemiah the Comforter

Nehemiah's name means "Jehovah comforts."[1] We know that the Holy Spirit is known as the Comforter. So in this season of restoration in Israel's history, Nehemiah served as a type of the Spirit of God. One of the assignments of the Spirit of God is to restore, heal, and help you get your life built back up. Nehemiah is a picture of the work of the Spirit of God in restoring us and healing us. Deliverance is a work of the Spirit. It is not the work of a man by which people come and get delivered.

In Matthew 12:28 Jesus said, "If I cast out devils by the Spirit of God, then the kingdom of God is come unto you" (KJV). So any work we do is not by might or power; it is by the Spirit of God. A man cannot deliver or restore you. It takes God to restore you. All a man can do is give you some medicine, pills, and try to cover up the damage done, most of the time getting you bound by something else. Only the Spirit of God can come into your life and take stuff out and build stuff up. Yes, He uses men like Nehemiah to be His hands and feet. He also uses the Word.

Let's now see what steps Nehemiah took in the natural to restore the physical walls and gates of Jerusalem. From these we can learn how to restore the spiritual walls and gates in our lives.

A Broken, Contrite Spirit

In Nehemiah 1:4 it says, "When I heard these words, I sat down and wept and mourned for days. Then I fasted, and prayed before the God of heaven." Notice that restoration always begins with a broken, contrite spirit and with prayer and fasting.

When a person's life is devastated, one of the best things he can do is to humble himself and weep. The Bible says, "The LORD is near to the broken-hearted, and saves the contrite of spirit" (Ps. 34:18). Fasting humbles the spirit, as I've mentioned previously. Fasting and prayer are foundations to restoration, especially with strong cases where there is a great amount of desolation. Weeping also shows godly sorrow, which, as 2 Corinthians 7:10 says, brings repentance that leads to salvation. You will notice that shortly after Nehemiah weeps and mourns, he petitions God with repentance on behalf of the people of Israel. (See Nehemiah 1:5–11.)

I often encourage people who come for deliverance whose lives are really devastated and messed up to spend some time fasting and praying. If your life has been seriously devastated, you should consider fasting as well. It doesn't mean you have to fast for forty days. You can just fast a day. Fast the day of the deliverance appointment. Fast one or two days. Fast three days. This is serious. You need the help of God. You need God to intervene, and if it's one thing that God responds to, it is a contrite spirit. He responds to people who humble themselves, and fasting brings humility. As a matter of fact, Jesus said that some kinds of demons only come out through prayer and fasting (Matt. 17:21).

Fasting also shows that you are serious. I have known people who want to be delivered and have a deliverance ministry encounter coming up, but they won't fast and pray. They won't do any prework. They're not really serious. They want people to pray for them and minister to them. They want a miracle, but they are not really serious enough about seeing restoration in their life to fast, pray, mourn, or do what they need to do to receive the level of help they need.

You have to be serious and believe that your life is worth living, worth fighting for, and worth being restored. Deliverance and restoration are for people who really want it—for those who see their condition and say, "God, only You can do this, and I am going to do what it takes. I'm going to press through. I'm going to get my healing."

Some people just give up. They want the easy way out. They don't want to do any praying. They want pastors, prophets, counselors, and intercessors to do all the work. They want us to use our anointing to set them free, but they won't read the Word, pray, repent, and fast. They keep coming to the altar with the same devils because they haven't spent any time humbling themselves.

Those who are serious about restoration are the ones who are on their way to it. This is not some, "Well, if God wants to do it, He'll do it. If not, that's OK." No. This is your life. Get in the right posture, and get ready for God to work a miracle of restoration in your life.

The Process of Rebuilding and Restoring

> When Sanballat the Horonite and Tobiah the Ammonite subordinate heard this, it deeply grieved them that there was a man coming to seek the welfare of the children of Israel.
>
> —Nehemiah 2:10

When you begin to seek restoration, the enemy will not like it. The devil will do everything in his power to stop it. He does not want your gates or your walls restored. He wants you to remain in the same shameful, desolate condition. So the first thing that happened in Nehemiah's story was that these enemies—Sanballat and Tobiah—began to plot and oppose the rebuilding of Jerusalem's walls. It was really none of their business because Nehemiah had legal orders from the king.

Just as the enemies of Israel liked seeing Israel in ruins, the devil also likes seeing you messed up. He will do everything in his power to discourage you, fight you, and hinder you. He'll use people. He'll use you against yourself. He'll use situations. It's not going to be easy. I do believe in miracles, and God can give you some miraculous breakthroughs. But sometimes restoration is a process. The effects of the enemy are moved out of our lives little by little.

The walls and gates that Nehemiah was rebuilding for Israel were not going to be rebuilt in a day. It was going to take some time. Not only did the people have the work of rebuilding in itself, but they also had to keep up a defense against the opposition, the enemies sent to frustrate them.

Stay focused; don't get distracted

One thing I love about Nehemiah is that he never allowed his enemies to distract him from what he had to do. Don't allow anything to distract you. Stay focused. Don't allow people—mama, daddy, sister, brother, dog, cat, or anyone—to cause you to lose your focus. This is your life. Don't let your enemies cause you to lose focus.

Sanballat even told Nehemiah he wanted him to come down and talk to him. Nehemiah said, "There's nothing to talk about. Who are you?" Nehemiah wouldn't leave his work to go and talk with Sanballat and his cronies because he was not willing to be distracted, even by something seemingly as good as negotiating.

Don't even negotiate with the devil. Your deliverance and restoration process is not up for negotiation. There is nothing to talk to him about. It's unfortunate that people, when they start moving toward deliverance, allow everything to distract them. They allow people and situations to stop them.

You cannot allow anything to distract you. You have to remain focused, committed, and dedicated to seeing every area of your life rebuilt and restored. Don't allow yourself to get caught up in other things that have nothing to do with your restoration.

Assess the situation

> So I went out by night by the Valley Gate toward the Dragon's Well and then to the Dung Gate, because I was inspecting the broken-down walls of Jerusalem and its burned gates.
>
> —Nehemiah 2:13

The first thing Nehemiah did, as he came upon the area needing repair, was survey the situation. Sometimes it's good to sit down and survey what your situation is. Write out what you have gone through. Have you been hurt? Have you been rejected? Have you been molested? Have you been abused? Have you been divorced? Do have a broken heart? Have you been through any traumatic situations? Are you bitter? Are you angry? What has happened in your life in the past?

Begin to look at what you are dealing with. It's good to know what you're dealing with because sometimes, if you are working with a Christian counselor or deliverance worker, they will be prompted by the Spirit of God to ask you, "What have you been dealing with?"

This is not the time to get religious and say that you have a silent prayer request. Prayer is not silent. Ask, and you shall receive! Seek, and you shall find. Knock! They that call upon the Lord…It's OK to tell someone what you are dealing with. Now sometimes it is shameful, but you ought to be able to trust the person who is praying for you. It is shameful a lot of the time what people have gone through. Sometimes the spirit of God will show ministers what it is. Other times you'll have to tell them. Some ministers or counselors have surveys or checklists of common issues or challenges people faced throughout their lives. They may ask things such as:

- "Have you been involved in the occult?"
- "Have you been rejected, hurt, or traumatized, or have bad things happened in your life?"
- "What is your major struggle?"
- "Do you have problems with your temper? Anger? Wrath? Lust?"
- "Have you had multiple relationships with people?"
- "Do you have difficulty making decisions or committing to a course of action?"
- "Have you been in and out of churches?"
- "Have you been in a physical accident?"
- "Has someone close to you died?"
- "Who or what has hurt you? Who has abused you?"

So again, it is good to be able to assess what you're dealing with in the spirit. It's good to have a target. You can do the same kind of surveying even in self-deliverance. There are some people who have made it a practice to journal and write out what they go through on a regular basis. Many times they are able to walk themselves through deliverance, keeping their hearts and minds clear and any breaches in their walls and gates closed up.

Be encouraged—God loves working in impossible situations

> But when Sanballat the Horonite, Tobiah the Ammonite subordinate, and Geshem the Arabian heard it, they laughed us to scorn, and despised us, and said, "What is this thing that you are doing? Are you rebelling against the king?"
>
> —Nehemiah 2:19

One of the first things the enemy will try to do is mock you and laugh at you: "You can't do this. You're not going to be successful. It's not going to work. You're not going to get healed and restored. You're messed up. It's too much. It's impossible." God loves impossible situations because He is the God of the impossible. Don't listen to the enemy. He'll do everything in his power to try to stop you, discourage you, and get you to turn back and quit.

I've known people who have become physically sick on the day that they gathered up enough courage to come for deliverance. Some start having migraine headaches. All kinds of crazy things start happening because the enemy wants to make them feel that the process of restoration is crazy and may not be for them right now. Nehemiah, representing the Comforter, shows us that the Spirit of God will never allow any person or anything to stop Him from His assignment to heal you and deliver you. He has been sent by God to be your helper.

Set a watch

> Nevertheless we prayed to our God, and, because of them, we set a watch for them day and night.
>
> —NEHEMIAH 4:9

Another thing you want to be sure to do throughout the process of restoration and healing is to set a watch against the enemy. Setting a watch is a principle of prayer and intercession through which you establish specific times for prayer and spiritual warfare. You can do this daily if necessary.

When the Israelites knew the enemy was trying to stop them, they set up watchmen on the walls to watch and alert the camp if the enemy tried to approach. They knew there was a chance that these enemies would literally attack them when they were trying to rebuild the walls. Watchmen are symbolic of intercessors, prayer warriors, and prophetic people. Watchmen are prophets. I believe one of the most powerful principles of restoration is to get connected to a church that operates in prayer, intercession, and the prophetic ministry. You need prophetic people to help pray for you.

Get a prayer partner. Get connected with a prophetic person, a watchman, who will watch with you, who will be faithful to pray you through the restoration process, and who knows how to intercede and stop the attacks of hell against your life. Don't try to do it by yourself. Find a mature, Spirit-filled believer and say, "Look. I'm going through deliverance. Can you pray for me? Can you help watch with me? I'm dealing with this." Solicit the support of an altar worker or your pastor. Get support from someone who will stand with you and watch and pray, because the enemy wants to sabotage what God wants to do in your life. And sometimes getting those one or two believers to pray with you can make all the difference. A threefold cord is not easily broken (Eccles. 4:12).

Haul away the rubbish

> And Judah said, The strength of the bearers of burdens is decayed, and there is much rubbish; so that we are not able to build the wall.
>
> —Nehemiah 4:10, kjv

When the walls were burned and torn down, piles and piles of rocks, stones, and wood—rubbish, refuse, and garbage—had to be hauled away. The people couldn't rebuild the walls until they carried away all the burned and broken stones and wood. The rubbish had to be carried out before the people could bring in new stones to rebuild the walls. Now this is a picture of deliverance. Rubbish represents unclean spirits. It represents junk and garbage that is in your life that needs to be taken out before you can be restored.

Notice it says, "The strength of the bearers of burdens is decayed." There was so much rubbish that the ones who were carrying the rubbish out got tired. I've prayed for people, casting demons out of them, for so long that they became too physically tired to receive any more deliverance even though there were demons still in them. They had so much rubbish in their lives. My altar workers and I have prayed for people for two or three hours. People had so much stuff that we were drained and they were drained. Even though we know that some people want it all out in one session, sometimes we have to split it up: "I'm tired. You're tired. Let's just stop it now. Come back again, and we'll work on it more." There was just too much spiritual rubbish.

Spiritual rubbish can consist of any number of demons. Here's the most common spiritual rubbish that remains in people's lives whose gates and walls have been made desolate:

- Addiction
- Anger
- Bitterness
- Brokenness
- Death
- Depression
- Fear
- Hurt
- Lust
- Occultism
- Oppression
- Pain
- Poverty
- Pride
- Rebellion
- Rejection
- Sadness
- Self-pity
- Shame
- Torment
- Unforgiveness
- Witchcraft

This is what deliverance is. Deliverance is the clearing-out process. It is the process for getting rid of the rubbish so that we can get the walls built back up. The Spirit of God will use the ministry of deliverance to clean out the rubbish, to clean out the demons, to clean out the uncleanness, and to get the garbage out of your life. It takes a lot of strength to do that. It takes deliverance workers who are strong in prayer, and you have to be strong enough as well. Don't force the deliverance session longer than what's necessary. If you're ministering, don't kill somebody trying to get them delivered. If you're the one receiving ministry, don't be the one who has to get out all the demons in one session. You're not competing for a trophy for being the World's Greatest Demon Buster.

Sometimes the Spirit of God will have you stop, and you won't feel the anointing to pray anymore. The Spirit of God will check you and say, "OK, let's stop." Then you can bless the person and let them know that sometimes the rubbish doesn't all get hauled away on one day. You have to follow the Spirit of God. Remember, deliverance is His work, and sometimes it happens little by little.

War and fight through the process

> Now when our enemies heard that this had become known to us and that God had brought their counsel to nothing, then we all returned to the wall, everyone to his work. After that day, half of my servants did the work while the other half handled the spears, shields, bows, and body armor. Commanders were appointed to support every house of Judah.
>
> —NEHEMIAH 4:15–16

Notice that half of them built and half of them were ready for war. This shows us that restoration is not all building; it's also warring. You will have to war and fight through the process. In the verses above we see that some of the servants took up spears, shields, bows, and body armor. We know shields represent the shield of faith. We also know the weapons of our warfare today are not carnal (2 Cor. 10:4); we war in the spirit realm. We have the sword of the Spirit, which is the Word of God.

Nehemiah and the Israelites had physical weapons because they were dealing with a physical wall, but we have spiritual weapons—the Word of God, confession, prayer, fasting, the shield of faith, the blood of Jesus, praise, worship, and so on. These are all weapons that you can use against the powers of hell. It's important for individuals going through deliverance, getting the rubbish removed, and getting the walls restored in their lives to dwell in an atmosphere of praise, worship, and the Word. They need to be speaking the Word, praying and fasting, staying in fellowship with a local church body, and walking in faith. They are learning how to war and fight and rebuild all at the same time.

Now, as I mentioned earlier, you may be new to spiritual warfare. That's why it's important to have someone stand with you who knows how to war and fight—intercessors, prophets, pastors, friends, and loved ones. Those people will stand with you, praying and warring against the attacks of the enemy on your behalf. Their experience in spiritual warfare tells them that the enemy will do everything in his power to stop you from being healed and restored, and they don't want to see that happen as much as you don't.

Understand that the battle is not yours

> Those rebuilding the wall and those hauling the loads were working with one hand doing the task, but with the other hand holding the weapon. For the builders, everyone had

> his sword bound to his side, even while rebuilding. The trumpet blower worked beside me.
>
> I said to the nobles, the rulers, and to the rest of the people, "The work is vast and over a large area. Since we are spread along the wall far from each other, assemble to us there at the place where you hear the trumpet sounded. *Our God shall fight for us.*"
>
> —NEHEMIAH 4:17–20, EMPHASIS ADDED

You need to get your Bible and underline that last sentence. You must understand that the battle is not yours. It belongs to God. It's His battle. God will fight for you! You are not alone. The whole principle here is that Nehemiah was undermanned. He said, "We are spread along the wall far from each other." They didn't even have enough men on the wall to properly defend it. But Nehemiah trusted that God had sent him and that no matter what was against him, he would prevail. One of the things you need to understand if you are going to have victory in warfare and deliverance is that if God is for you, who can be against you (Rom. 8:31)? No weapon formed against you shall prosper (Isa. 54:17). God is on your side. God wants to see you through, and He will help you fight.

Guard and protect the work

> So we labored in the work with half of them holding spears from sunrise to the rising of the stars. Likewise at the same time I said to the people, "Every man and his servant must lodge within Jerusalem. By night, they may be a guard to us; by day, a laborer for the work."
>
> —NEHEMIAH 4:21–22

We've touched on this already, but even while you are working to be restored, the work that you have accomplished thus far must be protected and defended against the enemy.

Maintain your gates by becoming a student of the Word

> All the people gathered together as one man in the area in front of the Water Gate, and they asked Ezra the scribe to bring the Book of the Law of Moses, which the Lord had commanded to Israel. On the first day of the seventh month, Ezra the priest brought the Law before the congregation of men, women, and all who could listen with understanding. In the area in front of the Water Gate, he read aloud from sunrise until midday to the men, women, and those who could understand. All the people listened attentively to the Book of the Law.
>
> —Nehemiah 8:1–3

Now, as I've highlighted, the Book of Nehemiah records the restoration of Jerusalem's gates. There were eleven gates around the city of Jerusalem, and each gate has a prophetic meaning—the Sheep Gate, the Dung Gate, the Valley Gate, the Fish Gate, the Water Gate, the Gate of Ephraim, and so on. Each one of them has prophetic significance to the gates in our lives, and each one of them is a type of something personal in an individual's life. Just as Nehemiah and the people restored each of these gates of Jerusalem, so you will restore the gates that have been desolated in your life.

Once you get restored, you must allow the Word of God to work in your life. You must become a student of the Word. You'll not be able to maintain your gates and walls without the Word. Restoration is not a "come, get healed, and go home" type of process. The Word of God is the only thing that can keep you and preserve you.

I've known people who have come for prayer and deliverance, but they were not desperate or determined enough to build a strong foundation by studying and reading the Word for themselves. They only wanted to come to church and hear a sermon. As a matter of fact, I remember that in the early days of Crusaders Church, we used to go to another ministry for deliverance. This ministry had a policy that if you did not come to hear the Word, they would not pray for you. Why? Because some people would time the service until the preaching was over and then get there just in time to receive prayer. Their rule was that if you can't sit through a message and don't have time for the Word, we don't have time for you.

Some people want to come and just get prayer: "You bless me." But they don't want to study, hear, or walk according to the Word. They just want someone to wave their hand over them and they receive a miracle. They don't want to pay the price of studying the Word of God.

But as I said: the Word of God is the only thing that can keep you. The reason Israel was in this condition in the first place was because the people walked away from the Law. That's why their gates and walls were destroyed. But Ezra came to bring them back, saying, "We're going to rebuild this city." However, you must remember that Israel is a physical type for what we have done and then for what we should do in the spirit. We need the Word of God in our lives.

The problem with Israel was that they always thought that because Jerusalem was the holy city and the temple of God was there, God would not allow their enemies to destroy them. But God is not concerned about physical stuff. Jerusalem was just a physical city and the temple was a physical building. God moved out of it and then sent the Babylonians to destroy it. God is not concerned about rocks and physical gates more than He is concerned about people. God is not concerned about some place being holy; He wants you to be holy.

Physical stuff can always be rebuilt or replaced. It's the spiritual that's the most important, because what happens in the spirit will affect the natural. If you are messed up in your spirit, you are going to be messed up in life. You can't change the external and not deal with the internal. Some people want to change their external environment, but if you are full of hate, it makes no difference if you are in a cardboard box or a mansion. You will still manifest demons and tear up the mansion.

The Word of God will transform you from the inside out and cause you to have the strength of character to maintain your restoration.

Rejoice and enjoy the fruit of your labor

> All the congregation who had returned from captivity made booths and lived in them. Not since the days of Joshua the son of Nun to that day had the children of Israel done so, and there was a tremendously great feast. And day by day, from the first day to the last day, he read from the Book of the Law of God. They celebrated the feast seven days, and on the eighth day there was a solemn assembly as required.
>
> —NEHEMIAH 8:17–18

This verse is describing the Feast of Tabernacles, which was a feast of ingathering and harvest. It was the most joyful of all the feasts. Bringing in the harvest signals that it's money time. It's time to celebrate.

Remember that Passover was very solemn because it represents coming out of Egypt. Pentecost was the firstfruits of the harvest, and there was some joy that accompanied that feast.

But during the Feast of Tabernacles, when the harvest came in, there was much joy and celebration. God commanded this feast. He told the people to go to Jerusalem for seven days and to rejoice.

God wants you to enjoy the fruit of your labor. You cannot work, work, work and never enjoy. You'll hate life. You have to have a harvest in your life.

After the harvest the people of Israel could rest until the planting season. It was vacation time. They had plenty of wine, wheat, and corn. They could rejoice. This feast is a picture of praise and worship and victory celebrations.

The point I want to make is this: when you get your walls restored and the rubbish out of your life, not only do you need to be in place where the Word is, but you also need to be in a place where there's celebration and joy. You need to be in a place of praise and worship. You need to be in the presence of God.

The Feast of Tabernacles shows that once we are restored, we become God's tabernacle. He dwells in us. Where the presence of God is, there is joy, rejoicing, and celebration. The joy of the Lord is our strength (Neh. 8:10).

You need the Word, and you need tabernacle. You need God's presence, God's anointing, and God's glory. You need joy, rejoicing, celebration, and harvest. You need to be in that kind of atmosphere. The Word, praise, and presence—those are the three things that result when you start getting restored.

When you start getting restored, you can start enjoying the Word. You can hear and understand the Word. You are able to rejoice and enjoy God's presence. When your life is all messed up and you are confused and tormented, it's hard to understand the Word. It's hard to walk in the Word. It's hard to enjoy God's presence. It's hard to enjoy joy and celebration. But once you are healed and restored, you can have life and have it more abundantly. You can have joy unspeakable and full of glory. You can have the Word of God in your life. You can be protected, and you can close every gate and every door to the enemy.

Authority Restored

Not only do gates in the Bible represent protection against the enemy, but they also represent authority. Remember that the elders, princes, and rulers would sit at the gate of the city. The gates were the place where judicial decisions were made. The town court was held there. So gates represent authority.

When your gates are restored, it means that your authority is restored. The devil no longer can do to you what he wants. When your gates are restored, whatever you bind on earth is bound in heaven, and whatever you loose on earth is loosed in heaven (Matt. 18:18). Your power to tread upon serpents and scorpions and over all the power of the enemy is restored. (See Luke 10:19.) People whose gates are messed up have no authority. The devil just does what he wants to do in their lives.

When you've been restored, your authority is restored. You can say, "No, Satan, you can't have my family, my finances, my body, or my mind. Sickness, I bind you. Poverty, I bind you. Depression, no. Sickness, no. Defeat, no. Lust, no. Perversion, no. Sin, no. Rebellion, no. Torment, no. Affliction, no. You cannot run my life. My gates are restored. Satan, I have power and authority over you."

> Violence shall no more be heard in your land, nor devastation or destruction within your borders; but you shall call your walls Salvation and your gates Praise.
>
> —Isaiah 60:18

Sent Ones

Not only was he a type of comforter, Nehemiah was also a picture of the apostolic anointing. Just as the Holy Spirit was sent by Jesus, Nehemiah was sent by God. And we have been sent as well to comfort, help, heal, and restore people. We now have an anointing on us.

In Isaiah 58 we are challenged to be repairers of the breach, to restore the broken foundations in other people's lives. Just as the restoration of Israel provided a lesson and strategy for us, so too will our restoration be a help and testimony to others of the faithfulness of God. You will be one whom others can ask to stand with them as they war and fight for their restoration.

This is the hope you can count on: You will be made whole. Your walls will be built back up and you will not be a city broken down and without walls. You'll be fortified and protected from the enemy, and you can live in safety and prosperity. The enemy will no longer be able to do what he wants to do with your life.

CHAPTER 10

THE RIGHT WAY TO HANDLE REJECTION

The sacrifices of God are a broken spirit; a broken and a contrite heart, O God, You will not despise.

—PSALM 51:17

GOING FORWARD AS a restored person back into real life, you must understand that you may face rejection and any number of troubling circumstances again and again. Jesus said, "In this world you will have tribulation. But be of good cheer. I have overcome the world" (John 16:33).

One of the things you learn in life is that when you are rejected, you will deal with that rejection in some way. Whether it is human or divine rejection, your spirit will react. Of course there are ways to handle rejection that are not productive and restorative, such as bitterness and anger. Then there are constructive ways to handle rejection that set you on a path to restoration and power over the enemy.

How to Deal With Rejection

In this chapter we are going to discuss five ways to properly deal with rejection of any kind. In the case of being rejected by God, you may have been involved with a lifestyle that God does not approve of, but it does not mean all hope is lost. You don't have to lose it all as Saul did. You can be set back on the right path. It all depends on how you handle it.

1. Ask why

Sometimes there are valid reasons for being rejected. All rejection is not from the devil. There are standards and requirements for participation in various areas in society. If you apply for a job but don't have the education or experience the employer is looking for, you may not get a response to your application. If you apply to Harvard but don't have the grades and they send you a rejection letter, don't go and write a manifesto on your Facebook page. Understand that this kind of rejection is valid and is nothing to get bent out of shape about.

Thousands of people get rejected every year from certain schools. That's why guidance counselors tell you to apply to more than one; then you have options. Sometimes a school will reject you because your grades don't meet its standard; sometimes a school may not have enough room to accept everyone who applies—there are only a certain number of student openings. A school could send you a rejection letter for a number of reasons, but again, there is valid rejection.

Remember, this type of rejection is not personal. It does not have to ruin your life. Just apply for another position or to another school, and keep moving.

There are also situations in church or in society where your character has to meet a certain standard in order for you to be accepted. You don't automatically have a right to it just because you want it. If you don't measure up to a certain set of qualifications, you can be turned down.

Sometimes people get rejected for no good reason. The rejection is unjust. You can be rejected through no fault of your own. You can be rejected because of your race, gender, or because somebody simply doesn't like you. Sometimes you're rejected because of jealousy.

Joseph was rejected by his brothers, and he was a righteous man. Not only did his brothers reject him, but they also sold him into slavery in Egypt. But understand, Joseph never allowed that rejection to destroy him. As a matter of fact, he began to discern that it was God who allowed that to happen to get him to Egypt. He took the time to examine his situation and see it through God's eyes. When he saw his brothers years later, instead of getting revenge, he forgave them. He didn't even let them remain afraid of him, though he had the authority to kill them. He said, "No, you're my brethren. I understand that it was God who did this. He has me here for a purpose."

Sometimes you have to stop and ask, "Why was I rejected?" Using discernment when you've been rejected can bring great deliverance and breakthrough to your life and to those around you, just as it did for Joseph. When you've been rejected, keep your heart pure, forgive, and start expecting supernatural breakthrough to come soon. You may get turned down for a job or an academic program, but what other thing is God trying to work in your favor?

We all have to respond to rejection. Joseph could have been bitter. He could have been angry. He could have been vindictive. But he wasn't, and God blessed him tremendously. Too many of us aren't able to handle rejection with a discerning heart. Instead of handling it with grace and forgiveness, expecting God to be working all things for our good, we take rejection personally. We become bitter and angry. This is why so many people need deliverance in this area—they allow rejection to darken their perspective. But we have a choice to handle rejection in a way that can take us from the prison to the palace, just as Joseph did. Our next promotion could be tied to how we handle rejection today.

2. Do well

We've already discussed God's rejection of Cain in chapter 2. If you recall, God rejected Cain's offering, but He accepted Abel's. Genesis 4:5–7 says, "But for Cain and for his offering, He did not have respect. And Cain was very angry and his countenance fell. The Lord said to Cain, 'Why are you angry? Why is your countenance fallen? If you do well, shall you not be accepted?'" In other words, God was saying, "I'm not rejecting you because of you. I'm rejecting you because of your offering. But if you do the right thing, I'll accept you." So it was nothing personal. Instead of Cain discerning the reason why he was rejected, he got angry and killed his brother.

Cain did not respond to rejection correctly, even though God told him, "If you do what is right, I'll accept you." Maybe he could have gone and changed his offering, brought the correct offering, and God would have accepted him. But he didn't do that. He allowed the rejection to lead him down a path of self-destruction—anger, bitterness, murder, and finally a curse.

Most people respond to rejection in this way, opening the door to spirits of anger, hatred, and sometimes even murder. But they could find out why they were rejected, reexamine the requirements, "reapply" with the right thing, and perhaps be accepted.

3. Seek to understand and obey the standard

As I have said, there is valid rejection. Sometimes people with the spirit of rejection have a difficult time discerning valid rejection from invalid rejection. There are standards in everyday life and with God that have to be adhered to. Rejections that come as a result of not meeting certain criteria are not personally set up against you. If you are rejected for a valid reason, it is not because you are unloved. There was just a requirement you didn't meet this time around. So here is where you need to seek to understand the requirement and figure out ways to obey it.

> My people are destroyed for lack of knowledge. Because you have rejected knowledge, I will reject you from being My priest.
>
> —Hosea 4:6

In essence, what God is saying here is, "If you are going to be My people, you will need to be knowledgeable. I need people who know Me, know My Word, and know My Spirit. I can't have people who say they belong to Me and are ignorant." This particular time Israel had rejected the knowledge of God. They rejected the word of God. They didn't want to keep God's standard. I am not saying God is going to reject you because you don't know every verse in the Bible. I'm simply saying that when you are part of God's people, one of the signs that you are His is that you have knowledge.

Paul wrote to Timothy, "Study to show yourself approved by God" (2 Tim. 2:15). God accepts people who study, people who know what is required and do it. He rejected Israel because the Israelites rejected knowledge. Basically they wanted to remain ignorant. Some people think that ignorance is a valid excuse for disobedience: "I didn't know fornication was wrong. I just figured God gave you all these desires." Or, "I didn't know I needed to turn in that form so that my application could be accepted." Whatever it is, people who have an understanding of what is required and do it will receive the benefits of what they are seeking approval for.

God said, "I will reject you from being My priest." In other words, God is saying, "You can't be a priest. You can't minister to Me or represent Me if you have no knowledge of Me. You're ignorant."

God gave the Israelites commandments so that they could know Him and have His wisdom and knowledge. But they rejected His commandments: "No we don't want this. This is too much. We don't want the responsibility of learning Your laws and learning Your Word. We just want the blessings. We don't want the responsibility of knowing." I've heard people say this about other areas in life too: "Oh, I didn't know it was going to take all this."

But maybe it does take a lot, and maybe it's worth it. Maybe you didn't have what it took the first time. Get familiar with what you need to know, regroup, go back to school, get some ministry training, find someone to be accountable to, and try again.

For life in the Spirit approval from God is everything. It is worth learning what He requires so that you can experience His glory on your life.

God said, "No, I can't accept ignorance! I'm raising up a new people who will know Me and My ways. I am going to put My law and My Word inside of them."

It is critical as believers, as saints, to understand that God has a standard. He doesn't accept everything. Yes, God is love, but He still doesn't accept just anything. Your employer doesn't accept just anything. The school you may want to attend doesn't expect just anything. The requirements have been made clear. Now it's up to you to abide by them so that you can experience the benefits God has set up for your successful life.

4. Accept that your acceptance comes only through Christ

Regardless of what's happening in the world, what opportunities we want, or what goals we want to achieve, the only reason that any of us receive true acceptance is not because God accepted us but because God accepted us through Jesus Christ. It was through His blood that we became acceptable.

Matthew 13:47–48 says:

> Again, the kingdom of heaven is like a net that was cast into the sea and gathered all kinds of fish. When it was full, they drew it to shore, sat down, and gathered the good into baskets, but threw the bad away.

That's rejection. The bad was thrown away. The word *reject* means "to refuse to accept...take for some purpose, or use; to refuse to hear, receive, or admit." It means "to cast off [discard or throw out as worthless]"[1]; or in other words, "to discard that which is useless or substandard."

See, God's standard is so perfect that there's no way you can meet it without the blood of Jesus. That's why you must always put your faith in Him. It's not because of what you can do or what you can't do. You could never be good enough for God. The only way you can be accepted is to be justified by faith. That's it. Without faith it's impossible to please Him (Heb. 11:6).

Anything that is not perfect, God does not accept. Only perfect people go to heaven. And you're not perfect on your own. You are only perfect because Jesus is perfect. You become righteous because of His righteousness. His perfection becomes your perfection. You are justified by faith in Him. Some may say, "Well, you know God would never reject me because I am a good person. I may not be a believer like you, but I don't believe God would reject me." Yes, He will.

God rejects everybody—including you, unless you come to Him through Christ and accept by faith His sacrifice on the cross. The blood of Jesus then covers you and allows you to be presented faultless before God. This is the only way you can be qualified and accepted by God.

> So shall it be at the end of the world. The angels will come out and separate the evil from the righteous and throw them into the fiery furnace. There will be wailing and gnashing of teeth.
>
> —Matthew 13:49–50

So here is another case of rejection. God rejects the bad, just as you reject bad things. If you get a bushel of apples, and there's a bad one in there, what do you do with it? You reject it. You don't just eat it. You are very careful about what you eat. If something is not fresh, if it's spoiled, you reject it. If the food is not right in the restaurant, you send it back. God is the same way; if something is not correct—if it is wicked, evil, or sinful—God rejects it.

The only one God accepts is Jesus; you cannot be accepted unless you're in Christ. Many of us have a hard time understanding this. We think this whole salvation message is about going to church and doing this and not doing that—though we should strive to do well as it is a sign of our love for God (John 14:15, 23) and a sign of growth. But don't put the cart before the horse.

Some may complain, "I don't see why you have to be saved and be in Christ. Why do you need Christ? What's wrong with being a Muslim or a Hindu?" You must realize it's not about that. No religion is good enough for God to accept.

God is perfectly holy, and His standard is much higher than ours. His standard is perfection. He gave the Law so that when we failed to keep it, we would realize our need for a Savior. He knew His commandments were impossible to keep. He wanted the human race to have faith that there was one coming who would die for our sins and impart righteousness and salvation to us through that faith. In the meantime the people of Israel took the blood of animals to cover their sins every year. But even then they believed there was one coming who would take away their sins—the Messiah.

Jesus told Nicodemus in John 3:16, "For God so loved the world that He gave His only begotten Son." The reason God gave His Son was because He loved you and He understood that the only thing that would get you to heaven is perfection. That's why you have to remain in Jesus. Your perfection is not based on what you do or what you don't do. Your perfection is measured by your being covered by the blood of Jesus. It's all about Jesus. Put your trust in Him!

5. Let your faith match your lifestyle

When you say, "I have faith," does your lifestyle reflect your faith? In James 2 the apostle talks about people who say they believe in the Lord, but their lifestyles are raggedy; they are living as if God has no standard. They don't know five scriptures and have no real spiritual knowledge, but yet they know the Lord?

I had an aunt like that. She just knew she knew the Lord, but she was as sinful as can be. When I got saved, I felt like I was David in the house of Saul. I thought she was going to kill me for getting saved. She told me, "Don't come around me with all that Bible stuff. I went to church when I was little." She was from a small town in Mississippi, and she would play the lottery. So when I would give her scripture, trying to win her to the Lord, she would take the numbers and use them to play the lottery. Of course, I'm thinking that I'm breaking through to her. She's asking, "What's that scripture again, 5:26? OK." I'm praising God, "Hallelujah! Lord, I'm breaking through." Please. I was not breaking through. She was using those chapter and verse numbers as numbers to play in the lottery.

There was another lady whom I called Auntie, though she was really only a close friend of the family. She was an organist. But six days of every week she was in the tavern, and then on Sunday she was playing the organ at her church. She did not miss a church service. So I asked her, "Auntie, you've been in the tavern all week. You're cussing. How is it that you are saved?" She got mad at me. I couldn't tell her anything! "What do you mean I'm not saved?" she said. "Oh, you think because you're with this little church now that you know more than me, right? I've been in church!"

There are a lot of people like that, you know. They go to church. They believe in God. But what about their works, their lifestyle? Does it really reflect the life of a true believer?

> What does it profit, my brothers, if a man says he has faith but has no works? Can faith save him? If a brother or sister is naked and lacking daily food, and one of you says to them, "Depart in peace, be warmed and filled," and yet you give them nothing that the body needs, what does it profit? So faith by itself, if it has no works, is dead. But a man may say, "You have faith and I have works." Show me your faith without your works, and I will show you my faith by my works.
>
> —James 2:14–18

Faith is not only about talking. It's also about doing. "You believe that there is one God; you do well. The demons also believe and tremble" (James 2:19). So I guess the devil is saved too, huh?

> Was not Abraham our father justified by works when he offered his son Isaac on the altar? Do you see how faith worked with his works, and by works faith was made perfect? The Scripture was fulfilled which says, "Abraham believed God, and it was reckoned to him as righteousness," and he was called the friend of God. You see then how by works a man is justified, and not by faith only.
>
> —James 2:21–24

In other words, the fact that Abraham would be willing to sacrifice his son proved that he had faith. He knew that if he killed his son, God would have to raise him up because he knew his son was the heir. That's how much faith he had in God. He knew that his son would live no matter what. His faith showed that he was a righteous man full of faith.

Faith saves you. But your faith will always have works attached to it. What you believe and put trust in—whether good or bad—is demonstrated by your lifestyle.

What God Accepts

> Then Peter began to speak, saying, "Truthfully, I perceive that God is no respecter of persons. But in every nation he who fears Him and works righteousness is accepted by Him."
>
> —Acts 10:34–35

We can't impress God. He doesn't accept us because of our positions, titles, or good looks. God looks at the heart. He is not concerned about your color, your language, or your position, but in every nation He is looking for people who fear Him and do what is right. That's who God accepts—people made righteous by the blood of Jesus, who then live that righteousness out in godly lifestyles.

God does not accept rebellious people, witches, warlocks, perverts, liars, cheaters, and thieves. No, God doesn't accept them—He is under no obligation to do so.

If you feel like God isn't accepting your prayers, look at your heart. If you feel like your prayers are not getting anywhere, look at your heart. If you feel like God is not accepting you, look at your heart. The Bible says, "A broken and contrite heart, O God, You will not despise" (Ps. 51:17). God accepts humility, contrition, fear (reverence), and righteousness.

That's why we can look at the life of King David and see that God accepted him even though he committed murder and adultery. God didn't reject him because God saw his heart and knew that David's behavior was not really like him at all. David was a man after God's own heart. David was a worshipper. He was a man who loved God. The sinful things he did were not really part of his character. Now there is no excuse for what he did. But when he repented, God corrected him and accepted him. Just because you make a mistake doesn't mean God is going to kick you out. God looks at the heart. Man looks on the outward appearance.

Our whole desire should be to live lives that are acceptable to God. What other people are doing is their business. We should want to live our lives so that God will accept them as a living sacrifices. Romans 12:1 says that we should present our bodies as living sacrifices—holy and acceptable to God.

I don't know about you, but I want my worship, prayer, life, giving, and service to be acceptable to Him through Jesus Christ and through the power of the Holy Spirit. That's what I live for.

God's rejection comes as a result of His holiness and righteousness. God will never reject you if you come to Him. He will in no way cast you out. If you come humbly and accept Him, He will accept you. He will never close the door on you, but He will not compromise His standards to accept a lifestyle that is against His Word.

Seeking wisdom, knowledge, and understanding after rejection is a healthy way forward after being restored. Rushing right in with spirits of anger, revenge, and self-pity will bring curses and not blessing. Many times with rejection there are opportunities to learn, grow, and try again.

CHAPTER 11

GOD OF THE OVERFLOW

Fear not, O land; be glad and rejoice: for the Lord *will do great things.*

—Joel 2:21, KJV

As you begin to receive healing from the devastation of rejection, and you have begun the rebuilding of the broken gates and walls in your life, you will have a new ability to sustain and dwell in the blessing and abundance of God. We cannot expect to be able to walk in the peace, joy, and prosperity of God when our lives have been desolated and left in ruins. With the help of the Spirit of God we first took out the rubbish and garbage—this is deliverance—and then we could begin rebuilding the gates and walls so that we have a defense against enemy. When our gates and walls are repaired, the enemy cannot not rob and spoil the blessings of God that are meant for us.

The passage in Joel 2:21–29 speaks of the restoration of Israel, but, again, it is a picture of what God will do in our individual lives when we come to Him seeking deliverance, healing, and restoration. Most of the time when we read these verses, especially verses 28–29—"And it will be that, afterwards, I will pour out My Spirit on all flesh; then your sons and your daughters will prophesy, your old men will dream dreams, and your young men will see visions. Even on the menservants and maidservants in those days I will pour out My Spirit"—we read it in terms of revival, evangelism, and the outpouring of the Holy Spirit. Pentecostals are especially familiar with these prophetic words when they are fulfilled in Acts 2.

This prophetic word of Joel is a word to Israel. The Israelites had experienced what is known as locust invasions. God would send these locusts—literal locusts, palmerworms, caterpillars, and cankerworms—that would sweep through the land and desolate the entire land. Historically these locust plagues came and ate up all of the crops. Because Israel was an agricultural nation, for the people to lose all of their crops to swarming locusts meant that they had no blessing and no finances. The locust plagues represented a curse. It's what God told them would happen if they broke their covenant with Him. In Deuteronomy 28 He said He would send the locust, and the locust did come and devoured the land. So in Joel 2 we find the Israelites in mourning. They were desolate and had experienced the judgment of God. But then God gave a word to Israel that He would restore to them the years that the locusts had eaten.

What this reversal shows us is that even though there may be desolation in our lives because of rejection, disobedience, or rebellion, God is merciful and will restore to us the time that was lost.

One of the things we learned about restoration is that when God restores something, He never gives back to you only what you lost. He gives back to you more than what you lost. You can see this in the story of Job. The Bible says that God blessed Job with twice as much as he had before he was attacked by the enemy (Job 42:12–13). Using the types and symbols represented in the Old Testament account of Israel's deliverance from desolation to restoration, we will explore what this means for you.

GOD WILL DO GREAT THINGS

> Fear not, O land; be glad and rejoice: for the LORD will do great things.
>
> —JOEL 2:21, KJV

That was the word to Israel. It is also a word to us. You need to receive that today. God doesn't want to do just anything in your life. He wants to do great things for you. *Great* means "something big, phenomenal, and amazing; something that's beyond the ordinary." Expand your faith to believe God, not just for enough, but to believe God for something great to happen in your life.

GOD WILL RESTORE FRUITFULNESS

> Be not afraid, ye beasts of the field: for the pastures of the wilderness do spring, for the tree beareth her fruit, the fig tree and the vine do yield their strength.
>
> —JOEL 2:22, KJV

When restoration comes into a person's life, God restores fruitfulness. Desolation, lack, and poverty represent a curse, but fruitfulness and abundance represent prosperity and restoration. God says that the vine and the fig tree yield their strength. What this tells us is that as God begins to restore strength to our lives, He gives us the ability to bring forth fruit to manifest abundance.

In the Bible we are considered trees. We are called trees of righteousness, the planting of the Lord (Isa. 61:3). In Mark 11:12–25 we find the story of when Jesus cursed the fig tree because it was barren. He was hungry and went to the fig tree. He saw that it had leaves but no fruit, so He cursed it and said, "May no one ever eat fruit from you again" (v. 14). The next day

His disciples saw the fig tree had withered up (v. 20). God curses unfruitfulness. Therefore barrenness and unfruitfulness represent the curse of God.

Because you are no longer under a curse, God wants to remove all barrenness and fruitlessness from your life. He wants you to bring forth fruit—the fruit of the Spirit: love, joy, peace, temperance, and so on (Gal. 5:22–23, KJV). He wants your life to be fruitful. One of the things about fruitfulness is that when you are fruitful, somebody else can eat from your tree. This is important. Your ability to bear fruit is not only for you. God blesses you to be a blessing to others.

GOD WILL OPEN THE WINDOWS OF HEAVEN OVER YOUR LIFE

> Be glad then, ye children of Zion, and rejoice in the LORD your God: for he hath given you the former rain moderately, and he will cause to come down for you the rain, the former rain, and the latter rain in the first month.
>
> —JOEL 2:23, KJV

What God is saying here is essentially, "I am going to open up the windows of heaven. I am going to rain upon the land." In the Bible rain is another symbol of blessing, fruitfulness, and abundance. A lack of rain upon a person's life is a picture of a curse, a picture of barrenness. It's a picture of desolation.

Don't ever believe that it is the will of God for you to be desolate. Don't ever believe it is God's will for the heavens to be closed over your life. It is the will of God to pour upon you not just rain but also the former rain *and* the latter rain. He will pour both upon you. He says, "I am going to give you an abundance of rain."

God Will Cause an Overflow to Occur in Your Life

> And the floors shall be full of wheat, and the vats shall overflow with wine and oil.
>
> —Joel 2:24, kjv

No matter what area you need to be restored in, when God does restore you in that area, He gives you an overflow, exceeding abundance, and more than enough. He opens up the windows of heaven and pours upon you so much that you don't have room enough to receive it.

Overflow is one of the signs of restoration. God says, in this particular case, that as a result of the rain, a great harvest would come upon Israel. The people would have so much wheat, wine, and oil that their storehouses would be full. Their vats would overflow with wine and oil. There would be abundance. Because the locust came and ate up everything, there was poverty. There was lack. But now God was saying to Israel, "I am a God of restoration. The locusts, cankerworms, palmerworms, and caterpillars have eaten up everything. You've been desolate, poor, and living in lack. You've been ashamed, and you haven't had enough. You've gone without. But great things are about to happen in your lives. I am going to pour so much upon you. I am going to cause so much fruit to come. The land that was barren is going to be fruitful. The wheat is going to come in its fullness. There will be wine and oil. I am going to cause an abundance, an overflow."

If you are believing God for restoration, you should also believe God for more now than you had before.

Some people are believing to have just enough: "If I have just enough, I'll be satisfied." "God, just let me make it through the week, through the year." But I believe that God is a God of overflow. Just as He did for Job, God will give you enough, and you will not only make it through the year, but you'll also have enough for years to come. Wouldn't it be nice if God gave you enough so you didn't have to worry about this year or the next year or the next year? God doesn't want you to make it through the year, and then when December 31 comes you say, "Whew! Man, that was close." He wants you to be run down and overtaken by His blessings.

God Will Restore What Was Lost in the Past

> And I will restore to you the years that the locust hath eaten, the cankerworm, and the caterpiller, and the palmerworm, my great army which I sent among you.
>
> —Joel 2:25, kjv

The pests in these verses are pictures of demons. Locusts, worms, caterpillars, and palmerworms are pictures of unclean spirits. In the physical they were literal locusts, cankerworms, caterpillars, and palmerworms that came in like an army God sent to devour their land and their crops after they had broken covenant. But in the spirit, for our lives today, they represent demon spirits that come to eat up the blessings of God in our lives. They come to devour. God wants us to be delivered from demons that want to devour our finances, our joy, our marriages, our families, our children, our ministries, and whatever we've acquired. These things come to eat up and devour even our time, but God says to you, "I am going to restore to you the years."

Now we know that you can't get time back, so He is not talking about physical years being restored. What He is saying is that all the crops the enemy devoured in the past years, He will restore back to you. This means He'll not only give you what comes in this year, but He'll also return to you what is owed to you from previous years.

You Will Be Satisfied

> And the floors shall be full of wheat, and the vats shall overflow with wine and oil.... And ye shall eat in plenty, and be satisfied, and praise the name of the Lord your God.
>
> —Joel 2:24, 26, KJV

Notice the words used in these verses: *full, overflow,* and *plenty.* God uses words that represent prosperity, such as *satisfied,* which means that you will have need of nothing. You will be satisfied. You will have so much, and this is not just referring to finances. This is also referring to joy, peace, righteousness, blessing, favor, anointing, grace, praise, and worship. It represents all the things that come with serving and worshipping God. You will be satisfied.

One of the things that God does not want is for us to live our lives unsatisfied. Being unsatisfied is not the blessing of the Lord. The blessing of the Lord makes rich and adds no sorrow with it (Prov. 10:22).

You Will Never Be Ashamed

> And ye shall eat in plenty, and be satisfied, and praise the name of the Lord your God, that hath dealt wondrously with you: and my people shall never be ashamed.
>
> —Joel 2:26, KJV

We've talked about a spirit of shame and reproach that comes upon a person who has been robbed and spoiled by the enemy. Well, God wants to do something for you in restoration to make sure that you'll never be ashamed. You'll never walk around with your head down. People will not look down on you. God wants to do something so wondrous in your life that it causes people who think they know you to be amazed. God can do something so great in your life that people will look at you, shaking their heads in disbelief. People who would have laughed at you, talked about you, made fun of you, criticized you, and gossiped about you will look at you as you are being restored, and they will scratch their heads, saying, "I don't know what it is, but God has really been good to you."

I want God to do something so great in my life through restoration, something so unbelievable that people will ask, "Are you the same person I used to know?"

God can bless you so much that it causes the doubters and naysayers to look at you and wonder what has happened in your life. Where you were once embarrassed about the state of your life, you are now confident in the One who lifted you up out of a horrible pit.

RESTORATION IS THE WORK OF THE HOLY SPIRIT

When God blesses a man, there's nothing people can do about it. When God restores a woman, there's nothing people can do about it. When God does something in your life, it makes no difference what people think or say. The apostle Paul wrote, "If God is for us, who can be against us?" (Rom. 8:31). When God pulls you up, man can't put you down. When God puts His glory and favor on your life, those who talked about you and looked down on you will be ashamed. God will exalt and promote you. He will set a table before you in the presence of your enemies; He'll anoint your head with oil and cause your cup to run over. (See Psalm 23.) And there's absolutely nothing anybody can do about it.

Restoration is not up to man. Man has no say so in this. This is between you and God. This is not up to somebody's vote or what anybody thinks, because if it were up to somebody else, you wouldn't even be in the room. They'd put you at the back of the line. You don't even qualify as far as people are concerned. You're the wrong size, wrong color, wrong gender, and wrong age, and you're in the wrong place. According to them, you don't fit at all. But God is not concerned about what man thinks about you. His restoration in your life is not the work of a man. It is the work of God. Man will let you down, but God will do what He said He is going to do.

The outpouring of the Holy Spirit will cause you to dream again

In Joel 2:28 the Lord begins to talk about the outpouring of His Spirit. Notice that the outpouring of the Holy Spirit on the Day of Pentecost was the beginning of restoration. This shows us that the work of restoration is the work of the Spirit of God. It also shows us that when restoration comes into your life, it brings the prophetic anointing. God says, "Your sons and your daughters shall prophesy."

One of the blessings God brings with restoration is a return of your ability to dream. He gives you back your vision. All of those dreams that left. All of the things that you thought would happen but never did. All the disillusionment. The heartache. The heartbreak. But with restoration God begins to restore your ability to dream again.

When you were a child, you dreamed. You had a great imagination. But as you grew older and encountered life, life began to knock out of you all the hopes, dreams, and visions you had. But when the Holy Spirit comes, you begin to dream again. You begin to have vision again. God begins to restore your ability to see into the future. No longer hopeless, you begin to see what you could not see before.

The Spirit of God, our Comforter, has been sent by God to bring restoration. When you get filled with the Holy Spirit and begin to walk in the Spirit, God is able to do something great and wondrous in your life.

BE FILLED WITH THE HOLY SPIRIT

Something we don't talk about much in the church anymore is being filled with the Holy Spirit and walking in the Spirit. There's a difference between Spirit-filled people and people who are not filled with the Spirit. People who are filled with the Holy Spirit know how to walk in the Spirit. He brings them to a level of faith and victory that they could not have without Him.

The Spirit of God makes a difference. People who are not filled with the Spirit live in the flesh. They can't even understand the things of God. It's difficult to explain spiritual things to unspiritual people. It's a different realm and a different dimension.

God wants us to receive the Holy Spirit because through Him the process of restoration can begin. God used the story of Nehemiah, whose name meant "the Comforter," to show that restoration begins when the Holy Spirit comes. He will start moving in our lives and performing signs, wonders, and miracles. There is no limit to a life that is filled with the Holy Spirit.

The infilling of the Holy Spirit is not just for speaking in tongues. It's supernatural empowerment to live a restored life full of miracles, healing, blessing, and favor.

Allow the Holy Spirit to be stirred up and to arise on the inside of you. When you begin to deal with situations, don't stand there scratching your head. Begin to lift your hands, pray in tongues, and allow the Holy Spirit to intercede for you. He will rise up inside of you with all authority, and you will overcome. When the enemy comes in like a flood, the Spirit of the Lord will lift up a standard against him (Isa. 59:19).

The Holy Spirit is not just for a church service. He's the Holy Spirit every day of the week. He's the Holy Spirit when you are dealing with an impossible situation. He's the Holy Spirit in sickness, disease, and death. He is the Holy Spirit for whatever comes. He's the Holy Spirit when the devil attacks your finances and your joy. He's the Holy Spirit who will cause you to break through every limitation and every barrier. He's the Holy Spirit who will cause you to leap over walls and leap over boundaries. And He's the Holy Spirit with whom nothing is impossible.

The body of Christ needs more people filled with the Holy Spirit. I'm not talking about people who speak in tongues every now and then. I'm talking about people who live and walk in the Spirit. People who are full of the Spirit and the anointing of God believe in the power of God no matter what the situation is.

When you are filled with the Spirit of God, you can truly say, "Greater is He that is in me than He that is in the world." (See 1 John 4:4.) The greater One lives inside of you.

CHAPTER 12

PRAYERS THAT DESTROY THE SPIRIT OF REJECTION

The righteous cry out, and the Lord *hears, and delivers them out of all their troubles.*

—Psalm 34:17

Prayer is a powerful weapon for believers who have a hatred for the works of darkness (Ps. 139:21). When you pray, you are breaking strongholds and enforcing the victory over Satan that Jesus won through His death on the cross. You are executing the judgments written against Satan through your prayers. You are reinforcing the fact that principalities and powers have been spoiled (Col. 2:15). This is why it is so unfortunate that there are so many believers who struggle with prayer. Many say they don't know how to pray. Some have become discouraged in prayer. This is why there are so many areas in their lives that are still under the oppression of the enemy.

The Lord taught me a long time ago the importance of praying the Word to overcome spiritual resistance to the plan of God for my life. The Holy Spirit has helped me understand many scriptures and how to use them in prayer so that I can continue to walk in victory.

When you base your prayers on the Word of God, it will inspire you to pray. Praying the Word of God will expand your ability to pray. It will stir up a spirit of prayer within you. We are told to pray with all kinds of prayers (Eph. 6:18). Praying the Word will cause you to pray many different kinds of prayers that you ordinarily would not have prayed. This will help to break the limitations off your prayer life. Reading, studying, and meditating on the promises of God will motivate you to pray. God has given many great and precious promises—promises to help you, to save and deliver you from the hand of the enemy, and to heal you and prosper you. It is through faith-filled prayer that you inherit these covenant promises (Heb. 6:12).

I have pulled together this collection of prayers that specifically address the demons operating within the spirit of rejection from deliverance and spiritual warfare books I've written over the years. There are also some new prayers that have come out of the flow of my ministering these principles to believers around the world. I believe that these prayers will prepare you to receive great deliverance and restoration from the desolation of rejection.

Prayers for Deliverance From Rejection

The lines have fallen to me in pleasant places; yes, I have a good inheritance (Ps. 16:6).

Lord, You are my light and my salvation. You are the strength of my life. I will not fear anything or anyone (Ps. 27:1).

The Lord is with me. I will not be afraid. What can man do to me (Ps. 118:6)?

You were despised and rejected. You are acquainted with my grief and sorrow. But by Your stripes I am healed of rejection (Isa. 53:3–5).

I believe and receive what You have said about me. Your truth sets me free from a spirit of rejection (John 8:32).

You have nailed my rejection to the cross. You have set me free; therefore I am free (John 8:36).

I declare that You have sanctified me with Your Word; Your Word over me is truth (John 17:17).

I am more than a conqueror (Rom. 8:37).

I am the righteousness of God in Christ Jesus (2 Cor. 5:21).

I am blessed with all spiritual blessings in heavenly places in Christ (Eph. 1:3).

I have been chosen by God from the foundation of the world (Eph. 1:4).

I am holy and without blame (Eph. 1:4).

I have been adopted as Your child according to the good pleasure of Your will (Eph. 1:5).

I am accepted in the Beloved (Eph. 1:6).

I am redeemed through the blood of Jesus (Eph. 1:7).

I am an heir (Eph. 1:11).

I am seated in heavenly places in Christ Jesus (Eph. 2:6).

I am the workmanship of the Lord, created in Christ Jesus for good works (Eph. 2:10).

I am a fellow citizen with the saints and members of the household of God (Eph. 2:19).

My inner man is strengthened with might by the Spirit of God (Eph. 3:16).

I am rooted and grounded in love (Eph. 3:17).

I am renewed in the spirit of my mind (Eph. 4:23).

I walk in love (Eph. 5:2).

I am filled with the Spirit of God (Eph. 5:18).

I am healed (1 Pet. 2:24).

I have been given exceedingly great and precious promises, that I may be a partaker of the divine nature of Christ (2 Pet. 1:4).

I am born of God; therefore I am victorious (1 John 5:4).

I am an overcomer by the blood of the Lamb (Rev. 12:11).

PRAYERS THAT INCREASE FAITH

I declare that I have uncommon, great faith in the power of Jesus Christ, faith that cannot be found anywhere else (Matt. 8:10).

Let it be to me according to my faith (Matt. 9:29).

I activate my mustard seed of faith and say to this mountain of sickness and disease in my life, "Be removed and go to another place." Nothing will be impossible for me (Matt. 17:20).

I have faith in God (Mark 11:22).

I go in peace because my faith has saved me (Luke 7:50).

I pray as Your anointed disciples prayed, "Increase my faith!" (Luke 17:5).

My faith will not fail (Luke 22:32).

Like Stephen, I do great wonders and signs because I am full of faith (Acts 6:8).

The just shall live by faith (Rom. 1:17).

The righteousness of God is revealed to me through faith in Jesus (Rom. 3:22).

I am justified by my faith in Jesus (Rom. 3:26).

By faith the promises of God are sure to me, the seed of Abraham (Rom. 4:16).

I will not stagger at the promises of God through unbelief, but I will stand strong in the faith, giving glory to God (Rom. 4:20).

I have access by faith to the grace of God (Rom. 5:2).

My faith increases the more I hear, and I hear by the Word of God (Rom. 10:17).

My faith is not in the wisdom of men but in the power of God (1 Cor. 2:5).

The Spirit of God has given me the gift of faith (1 Cor. 12:9).

I am established and anointed by God (2 Cor. 1:21).

No man has dominion over my faith. I stand by faith (2 Cor. 1:24).

I walk by faith and not by sight (2 Cor. 5:7).

I am a child of Abraham because I have faith (Gal. 3:7).

By faith I receive the promises of God in my life (Gal. 3:22).

I am a child of God because I have faith in Christ Jesus (Gal. 3:26).

Because of my faith in Jesus I have boldness and confident access to approach God (Eph. 3:12).

I take the shield of faith and quench all the fiery darts of the wicked one (Eph. 6:16).

I am raised to life through faith in Christ (Col. 2:12).

I put on the breastplate of faith and love (1 Thess. 5:8).

I will not suffer shipwreck in my life because I have faith and a good conscience (1 Tim. 1:19).

I obtain for myself good standing and great boldness in my faith in Christ Jesus (1 Tim. 3:13).

I will not be sluggish. I will imitate those who through faith and patience inherit the promises of God (Heb. 6:12).

I declare that I feel the substance and see the evidence of the things for which I have faith (Heb. 11:1).

I see through the eyes of faith the promise of things afar off. I am persuaded of their reality. I embrace them, knowing that I am a stranger and pilgrim on this earth (Heb. 11:13).

I will forsake any bondage that seeks to entrap me, looking forward by faith and setting my eyes on Him who is invisible (Heb. 11:27).

I decree and declare that by faith I will walk through my trials on dry ground, and my enemies will be drowned (Heb. 11:29).

I will encircle the immovable walls in my life, and by my faith those walls will fall down (Heb. 11:30).

I will subdue kingdoms, administer justice, obtain promises, and stop the mouths of lions because of my faith (Heb. 11:33).

I will stand firm and not waver. I will come boldly before God, asking in faith (James 1:6).

My faith is alive (James 2:17).

I will show my faith by the works I do (James 2:18).

I declare that my faith works together with my works, and by my works my faith is made perfect (James 2:22).

I pray the prayer of faith, and I will see the sick saved and raised up (James 5:15).

My faith and hope are in God (1 Pet. 1:21).

Prayers for Boldness and Courage

I will be strong and courageous; I will not be afraid, for the Lord is with me wherever I go (Josh. 1:9).

I will be courageous to keep and do all that the Lord has told me (Josh. 23:6).

I will deal courageously, and the Lord will be with me (2 Chron. 19:11).

I will wait on the Lord and be of good courage; He will strengthen my heart (Ps. 27:14).

I am bold as a lion (Prov. 28:1).

Let men see my boldness and know that I have been with Jesus (Acts 4:13).

Lord, grant me the boldness that I may speak forth (Acts 4:29).

Let me be filled with the Holy Spirit so that I may speak the Word of God with boldness (Acts 4:31).

I have boldness and access with confidence by faith in Christ (Eph. 3:12).

Lord, I pray with all prayers and supplication that I may open my mouth boldly to make known the mysteries of the gospel (Eph. 6:19).

Let me be much bolder to speak the Word without fear (Phil. 1:14).

I have great boldness in the faith of Christ Jesus (1 Tim. 3:13).

I have much boldness in Christ (Philem. 8).

I come boldly to the throne of grace, that I may obtain mercy and find grace to help in time of need (Heb. 4:16).

I have boldness to enter the holy place by the blood of Jesus (Heb. 10:19).

I boldly say, "The Lord is my helper; therefore I will not fear what man will do to me" (Heb. 13:6).

I will have boldness on the Day of Judgment, because as He is, so am I in this world (1 John 4:17).

PRAYERS FOR SEXUAL PURITY

In the name of Jesus I renounce all sexual sins that I have been involved with in the past, including fornication, masturbation, pornography, perversion, fantasy, and adultery.

In the name of Jesus I break all curses of adultery, perversion, fornication, lust, incest, rape, molestation, illegitimacy, harlotry, and polygamy.

In the name of Jesus I command all spirits of lust and perversion to come out of my stomach, genitals, eyes, mind, mouth, hands, and blood.

In the name of Jesus I release the fire of God to burn out all unclean lust from my life.

In the name of Jesus I break all ungodly soul ties with former lovers and sexual partners.

In the name of Jesus I cast out all spirits of loneliness that would drive me to ungodly sexual relationships.

In the name of Jesus I command all spirits of hereditary lusts from my ancestors to come out.

In the name of Jesus I command all spirits of witchcraft that work with lust to leave.

In the name of Jesus I take authority over my thoughts and bind all spirits of fantasy and lustful thinking.

In the name of Jesus I cast out all marriage-breaking spirits of lust that would break covenant.

In the name of Jesus I cast out and loose myself from any spirit spouses and spirits of incubus and succubus.

In the name of Jesus I cast out all spirits of perversion, including Moabite and Ammonite spirits of lust.

I receive the spirit of holiness in my life to walk in sexual purity (Rom. 1:4).

I am crucified with Christ. I mortify my members. I do not let sin reign in my body, and I will not obey its lust (Rom. 6:6–12).

I present my body to the Lord as a living sacrifice (Rom. 12:1).

My members are the members of Christ. I will not let them be the members of a harlot (1 Cor. 6:15).

I loose myself from the spirit of the world, the lust of the flesh, the lust of the eyes, and the pride of life. I overcome the world through the power of the Holy Spirit (1 John 2:16).

PRAYERS AGAINST LEVIATHAN

In the name of Jesus I break all curses of pride and Leviathan from my life.

Bring down the proud demons that have exalted themselves against Your people.

God, You resist the proud. Your power is against the high ones who have rebelled against You.

Break the pride of Leviathan's power (Lev. 26:19).

Raise up a watch over Leviathan (Job 7:12).

Smite through Leviathan with Your understanding (Job 26:12).

Cast abroad the rage of Your wrath and abase Leviathan (Job 40:11).

Look on Leviathan and bring him low. Tread him down in his place (Job 40:12).

Break the teeth of Leviathan and pluck the spoil out of his mouth (Job 41:14).

I strip the scales of Leviathan and take away his armor (Job 41:15; Luke 11:22).

Let not the foot of pride come against me (Ps. 36:11).

O Lord, break the heads of the dragons in the waters (Ps. 74:13).

Crush the heads of Leviathan in pieces (Ps. 74:14).

O Lord, render to Leviathan what he deserves (Ps. 94:2).

Let not Leviathan oppress me (Ps. 119:122).

Let not the proud waters go over my soul (Ps. 124:5).

I rebuke and destroy every trap the devil has set for me (Ps. 140:5).

Punish Leviathan, the piercing serpent, even Leviathan the crooked serpent, with Your fierce, great, and strong sword (Isa. 27:1).

Break the crown of pride (Isa. 28:1).

Let the waters of the deep be dried up, and destroy every spirit of Leviathan (Isa. 44:27).

Let the proud spirits stumble and fall (Jer. 50:32).

I call for a drought upon Leviathan's waters (Jer. 50:38; 51:36).

PRAYERS THAT BREAK THE SPIRIT OF PRIDE

I command the spirit of pride to cease its persecution of the poor.

Let the pride of Israel be broken in the name of Jesus.

The Lord is above the spirit of the proud (Exod. 18:11).

The Lord will break the power of pride; He will make my heavens like iron and my earth like bronze (Lev. 26:19).

I will not talk proudly and will let no arrogance come from my mouth (1 Sam. 2:3).

Like King Hezekiah, let prideful leaders humble themselves so that the wrath of the Lord does not come upon the people (2 Chron. 32:26).

Thank You, Lord, that You turn me from my deeds and conceal my pride from me so that my soul may be kept back from the pit and my life from perishing by the sword (Job 33:17–18).

Lord, I break the spirit of pride. Please answer when I cry out (Job 35:12).

Let that spirit be caught in the plots it has devised (Ps. 10:2).

The Lord will bring down haughty looks (Ps. 18:27).

Let not the foot of pride come against me, and let not the hand of the wicked drive me away (Ps. 36:11).

I do not respect the proud or those who turn aside to lies. I make the Lord my trust (Ps. 40:4).

Pride will not serve as my necklace, nor will violence cover me like a garment (Ps. 73:6).

The Lord will not endure a haughty look and a proud heart (Ps. 101:5).

Lord, my heart is not haughty (Ps. 131:1).

I fear the Lord; therefore I hate evil, pride, arrogance, and the evil way. I hate the perverse mouth (Prov. 8:13).

I rebuke the shame that comes from a spirit of pride (Prov. 11:2).

I come against strife that comes with the spirit of pride (Prov. 13:10).

The proud in heart are an abomination to the Lord. Let them not go unpunished (Prov. 16:5).

I break the spirit of pride, so that I will not fall and be destroyed (Prov. 16:18).

I come against the spirit of the proud and haughty man who acts with arrogant pride (Prov. 21:24).

I will not be wise in my own eyes (Prov. 26:12).

I will let another man praise me, and not my own mouth; a stranger, and not my own lips (Prov. 27:2).

I break the spirit of pride. It will not bring me low. I will have a humble spirit (Prov. 29:23).

Let the Lord halt the arrogance of the proud and lay low the haughtiness of the terrible (Isa. 13:11).

I break the pride of Moab. It shall no longer be proud of its haughtiness, pride, and wrath. The lies it speaks will not be so (Isa. 16:6).

Lord, bring dishonor to the spirit of pride (Isa. 23:9).

As a swimmer reaches out to swim, Lord, spread out Your hands in their midst and bring down the prideful and their trickery (Isa. 25:11).

Let the crown of pride, the drunkards of Ephraim, be trampled underfoot (Isa. 28:3).

May the Lord ruin the pride of Judah and the great pride of Jerusalem (Jer. 13:9).

Hear and give ear, spirit of pride. The Lord has spoken (Jer. 13:15).

Let the most proud stumble and fall, and no one raise him up. Let the Lord kindle a fire in his cities, and it will devour all around him (Jer. 50:32).

Those who uphold Egypt will fall; the pride of her power will come down, and those within her shall fall by the sword (Ezek. 30:6).

Those who walk in pride will be put down by the King of heaven (Dan. 4:37).

I break pride off of my life in the name of Jesus. I will not stumble in my iniquity as Israel, Ephraim, and Judah did (Hosea 5:5).

The spirit of pride will not rule me. I shall not be desolate in the day of rebuke (Hosea 5:9).

Let them not testify to His face then go on not returning to the Lord their God (Hosea 7:10).

Let all their cities and everything in them be given to their enemies (Amos 6:8).

Let not the pride of my heart deceive me. I have been brought low to the ground (Obad. 3).

The spirit of pride will not cause me to be scattered (Luke 1:51).

I dare not class myself or compare myself with those who commend themselves. They are not wise (2 Cor. 10:12).

I will not be puffed up with pride and fall into the same condemnation as the devil (1 Tim. 3:6).

The Lord resists the proud. Let me be like the humble one who receives grace from God (James 4:6).

I break the spirit of the pride of life, for it is not of the Father but is of the world (1 John 2:16).

HEALTH AND HEALING DECLARATIONS

By the stripes of Jesus I am healed. He took my sickness; He carried my pain. I believe it is the will of God for me to be healed.

In the name of Jesus I break every curse of infirmity, sickness, and premature death off of my body.

In the name of Jesus I break every curse of witchcraft and destruction over my body from both sides of my family.

In the name of Jesus I speak to every sickness in my body, and I command it to leave.

In the name of Jesus I speak to diabetes, high blood pressure, cancer, heart attack, stroke, and multiple sclerosis. Be removed and cast into the sea.

I speak to heart, kidney, back, lung, and liver problems. Be removed and cast into the sea.

I speak to blood, skeletal, and bone conditions. Be removed and cast into the sea.

I speak to lupus and every other disease. I command you to leave my body.

Every hidden sickness and every hidden disease, in the name of Jesus I command you to leave my body.

Arthritis, pain, and rheumatism, you must go in the name of Jesus.

In the name of Jesus I command all pain to leave my body. In the name of Jesus I come against skin conditions.

In the name of Jesus I tell infections to come out of my body.

In the name of Jesus I speak to breathing conditions, asthma, hay fever, sinusitis, chest congestion, and pneumonia and tell them to come out of my body.

Joint conditions and pain must go in the name of Jesus. I come against any conditions and infirmities that affect me as a woman—lupus, fibroid cysts, and tumors in the female organs. I command those tumors to die! In the name of Jesus I loose the fire of God to burn them out.

I come against nervous conditions, insomnia, and acid reflux. God has not given me the spirit of fear, but of love, power, and a sound mind.

Heart and circulatory conditions, irregular heartbeat, angina, and stroke must leave my body. I am the temple of the Holy Spirit. Be gone in the name of Jesus.

I speak to digestive disorders and allergies to certain food. You have no place in my body. You must go in the name of Jesus.

In the name of Jesus I break any and all addictions to pain pills.

Corroded disks; slipped disks; spine, back, and neck problems—be realigned and put back in place in the name of Jesus.

In the name of Jesus I release miracles of healing in my body.

I believe God for miracles of healing in my life and in my family wherever I go.

Thank You, Lord, for healing me and delivering me from all sickness and all pain.

I speak to every condition: you must obey.

I speak to miracles, healings, signs, and wonders. Be released into me in Jesus's name.

I thank You, Lord, that health and healing are coming now.

PRAYERS THAT CAST OUT THE SPIRIT OF INFIRMITY

Forgive me, Lord, for allowing any fear, guilt, self-rejection, self-hatred, unforgiveness, bitterness, sin, pride, or rebellion to open the door to any sickness or infirmity. I renounce these things in the name of Jesus.

In the name of Jesus I break, rebuke, and cast out any spirit of cancer that would attempt to establish itself in my lungs, bones, breast, throat, back, spine, liver, kidneys, pancreas, skin, or stomach.

In the name of Jesus I rebuke and cast out all spirits causing diabetes, high blood pressure, low blood pressure, heart attack, stroke, kidney failure, leukemia, blood disease, breathing problems, arthritis, lupus, Alzheimer's, or insomnia.

I break all curses of sickness and disease, and I command all hereditary spirits of sickness to come out.

In the name of Jesus I cast out any spirit of infirmity that came into my life through pride.

In the name of Jesus I cast out any spirit of infirmity that came into my life through trauma or accidents.

In the name of Jesus I cast out any spirit of infirmity that came into my life through rejection.

In the name of Jesus I cast out any spirit of infirmity that came into my life through witchcraft.

In the name of Jesus I command every germ or sickness that touches my body to die.

In the name of Jesus I rebuke any sickness that would come to eat up my flesh (Ps. 27:2).

No sickness or plague will come near my dwelling (Ps. 91:10).

Jesus carried my sickness and infirmities (Matt. 8:17).

I loose myself from every infirmity (Luke 13:12).

I am redeemed from every curse of sickness and disease (Gal. 3:13).

Prayer for a New Heart

Heavenly Father, I thank You for a new heart and a new spirit that You put inside of me. I will guard my heart. I will guard my mind. I will guard my thoughts. I will not entertain unclean thoughts or impure thoughts. I will not allow them to be planted in my mind and take root in my heart. Satan, I bind you. I will not allow you to put uncleanness and perversion in my heart. I keep my heart clean. Thank You, Lord, for delivering me from every unclean spirit that will try to operate in my heart. I bind and rebuke all uncleanliness from my mind from my heart in Jesus's name.

Rebuking the Spirits That Attack the Mind

Put your hand on your forehead and declare:

In the name of Jesus I take authority over all mind control and all spirits that would attack my mind. In the name of Jesus I bind and rebuke the spirit of passivity. In Jesus's name I rebuke fornication and uncleanness from my mind. My mind belongs to God. I cover my mind with the blood of Jesus. I rebuke all unclean thoughts from my mind. In the name of Jesus I let pure thoughts, holy thoughts, and clean thoughts come into my mind.

RESTORATION DECLARATIONS

It's restoration time in my life.

I believe that God is a restorer.

I believe that God is a God of plenty, a God of the overflow, a God of abundance, and a God of outpouring.

I believe the Lord will do great things in my life, no matter what it looks like now.

I believe that God will restore my life and give me more than I've ever had before.

In the name of Jesus I believe I will receive an overflow of blessing, favor, and prosperity in my life.

PRAYER FOR RESTORATION

I believe You, God, for total restoration in my life. Lord, You know every part of my life. You know every breach, every wall, and every gate. Lord, You know the condition of my walls and gates. I ask You now to restore any breaches in any area of my life. Any area that the enemy has access to, let it be closed; let it be repaired. Let it be restored.

Lord, I pray that any rubbish in my life would be removed. I open my life up to the Holy Spirit—my comforter, my builder, and my helper. I pray for complete restoration of every wall and every gate in my life. In the name of Jesus let every gate of my mind and my emotions be healed and restored.

Thank You, Lord, for repairing my life. I pray for any desolation in my life from my past to be restored and to be healed. I want to be made whole, Father.

I want to be delivered, set free, and made whole. I believe that the Holy Spirit is working in my life.

I thank You for the word of the Lord. I will receive it. I will hear it. I will walk in it. Thank You, Lord, for Your presence and Your glory. I will rejoice and enjoy Your presence and Your glory. Lord, I thank You for giving me life, and that more abundantly. Thank You, Lord, that every wall and every gate in my life is being restored through the Holy Spirit. I pray this in Jesus's name. Amen.

DECLARING GOD'S ACCEPTANCE THROUGH CHRIST

Through Jesus Christ and through His blood, by faith in Him, I have been made acceptable to God.

I have perfect righteousness because I have His righteousness.

God accepts me because of what Jesus did, not because of my works.

God is holy. His standard is perfection. Nothing less will do. I am perfected through the sacrifice of Jesus, and my lifestyle and works will show my faith.

Holiness and righteousness are God's standards. I commit my life to a life of holiness and righteousness; if I make a mistake, I know His blood will cleanse me. But my goal is that in Christ I will live a crucified lifestyle. My prayer, my praise, my worship, and my life will be acceptable to God through His Son Jesus Christ.

PRAYER FOR ACCEPTANCE FROM GOD

Lord, I love You. Accept my worship. Accept my prayer. Accept my life. Accept my ministry to You. Accept my service. Accept my giving. I present it all to You.

Accept it, O God. My life is my sacrifice to You, O God. Accept it through Jesus Christ.

I pray that my life will be acceptable to You, that it would come up into Your nostrils as a sweet-smelling savor. Let my life be pleasing to You, O God. I want to please You, Lord.

I will not compromise. I will not accept anything in my life that is unrighteous, ungodly, and evil. In the name of Jesus I will not lower my standard for any person or any teaching. I will keep my standard high. In Jesus's name I will have a standard of holiness and righteousness all the days of my life.

PRAYER OF THANKSGIVING

Thank You, Father. I believe today is the day for restoration. God, do wondrous things in my life. I will not be ashamed. I will be blessed above my past and my present. Thank You, Lord, that You are the God of restoration, abundance, and overflow. I believe the best is yet to come. In Jesus's name I pray this. Amen.

NOTES

Chapter 1
How Does Rejection Enter?

1. Noel and Phyl Gibson, *Excuse Me, Your Rejection Is Showing* (Lancaster, UK: Sovereign World Ltd., 1992).
2. Chuck D. Pierce and Robert Heidler, *A Time to Prosper* (Ventura, CA: Regal, 2013), 119.
3. *Merriam-Webster Online*, s.v. "trauma," accessed April 8, 2016, http://www.merriam-webster.com/dictionary/trauma.

Chapter 2
Rejected by God?

1. *Merriam-Webster Online*, s.v. "reprobate," accessed May 4, 2016, http://www.merriam-webster.com/dictionary/reprobate.

Chapter 3
Demonic Manifestations of Rejection

1. Win Worley, *Rooting Out Rejection and Hidden Bitterness* (n.p.: WRW Publications LTD, 1991), 2, as viewed at Hegewisch Baptist Church, "Reversing the Rejection Syndrome," accessed April 8, 2016, http://hbcdelivers.org/reversing-the-rejection-syndrome/. Used by permission of WRW Publications.
2. *American Heritage Dictionary of the English Language*, fifth edition, s.v. "megalomania," as quoted at FreeDictionary.com, accessed April 11, 2016, http://www.thefreedictionary.com/megalomania.
3. John Eckhardt, *God's Covenant With You for Deliverance and Freedom* (Lake Mary, FL: Charisma House, 2014), 36.
4. Richard Ing, *Spiritual Warfare* (New Kensington, PA: Whitaker House, 1996), 38.
5. Frank and Ida Mae Hammond, *Pigs in the Parlor* (Kirkwood, MO: Impact Christian Books, 1973, 2010), 141.
6. Ing, *Spiritual Warfare*, 49–50.

Chapter 4
Fear and Paranoia

1. John Eckhardt, *Deliverance and Spiritual Warfare Manual* (Lake Mary, FL: Charisma House, 2014), 223.
2. *Fausset's Bible Dictionary*, Electronic Database, copyright © 1998 by Biblesoft, s.v. "Emim."
3. Blue Letter Bible, s.v. "Hittite," accessed April 11, 2016, https://www.blueletterbible.org/lang/lexicon/lexicon.cfm?Strongs=H2850&t=KJV/.
4. Phobia Source, "What Are Phobias?," accessed April 11, 2016, http://www.phobiasource.com/what-are-phobias/.
5. Ibid.
6. This list is compiled from Phobia Source, "Phobia List," accessed April 11, 2016, http://www.phobiasource.com/phobia-list/.

Chapter 5
The Kingdom of Perversion

1. Blue Letter Bible, s.v. "*porneia*," accessed April 13, 2016, https://www.blueletterbible.org/lang/lexicon/lexicon.cfm?Strongs=G4202&t=KJV.
2. *Merriam-Webster Online*, s.v. "wicked," accessed April 14, 2016, http://www.merriam-webster.com/dictionary/wicked.
3. *Merriam-Webster Online*, s.v. "covetous," accessed April 14, 2016, http://www.merriam-webster.com/dictionary/covetousness.
4. *Merriam-Webster Online*, s.v. "malice," accessed April 14, 2016, http://www.merriam-webster.com/dictionary/malice.
5. *Merriam-Webster Online*, s.v. "envy," accessed April 14, 2016, http://www.merriam-webster.com/dictionary/envy.
6. *Merriam-Webster Online*, s.v. "insolent," accessed April 14, 2016, http://www.merriam-webster.com/dictionary/insolent.
7. Ibid.
8. BibleHub.com, s.v. "*astorgos*," accessed April 14, 2016, http://biblehub.com/greek/794.htm.

Chapter 6
Pride: The Spiritual Blocker

1. Gibson, *Excuse Me, Your Rejection Is Showing*, 38.
2. Steve Bell, "Spirit of Leviathan," accessed April 14, 2016, http://prideisamonster-leviathan.com/7155.html.

3. Ron Phillips, *Everyone's Guide to Demons and Spiritual Warfare* (Lake Mary, FL: Charisma House, 2010), 148.
4. Colin Urquhart, "Defeating the Leviathan Spirit," ColinUrquhart .com, accessed April 14, 2016, http://www.colinurquhart.com /Article/19/Defeating-the-Leviathan-Spirit.aspx.
5. Phillips, *Everyone's Guide to Demons and Spiritual Warfare*, 148–149.

CHAPTER 7
THE SPIRIT OF INFIRMITY

1. Chris N. Simpson, "Freedom From the Deep Hurts of Rejection," NewWineMedia.com, accessed April 14, 2016, http://www.new winemedia.com/pastorchris/print/Chris_Simpson-Freedom_From _Deep_Hurts_Of_Rejection.pdf. Used by permission of New Wine Media.
2. Spiritual roots of disease information has also been adapted from Life Application Ministries, "Are Some Dis-eases a Spiritual Condition?," accessed May 5, 2016, http://www.lifeapplication ministries.org/root.htm.
3. Ibid.
4. Ibid.
5. Ibid.
6. The Body of Christ Deliverance Ministry, "The Roots of Disease: General Overview," accessed May 25, 2015, http://www.thebocdm .com/the-roots-of-disease.html.
7. Life Application Ministries, "Are Some Dis-eases a Spiritual Condition?"
8. Ibid.
9. BibleHub.com, s.v. "*Marah*," H4785, accessed May 5, 2016, http://biblehub.com/hebrew/4785.htm.
10. BibleHub.com, s.v. "*marah*," H4784, accessed May 5, 2016, http://biblehub.com/hebrew/4784.htm.

CHAPTER 8
REJECTION MUST GO!

1. BlueLetterBible.com, s.v. "*ekballō*," G1544, accessed May 6, 2016, https://www.blueletterbible.org/lang/Lexicon/Lexicon.cfm?strongs =G1544&t=KJV.

CHAPTER 9
REBUILDING THE GATES AND WALLS

1. Blue Letter Bible, s.v. "Něchemyah," accessed April 15, 2016, https://www.blueletterbible.org/lang/lexicon/lexicon.cfm?Strongs=H5166&t=kjv.

CHAPTER 10
THE RIGHT WAY TO HANDLE REJECTION

1. *Merriam-Webster's Online*, s.v. "reject," accessed April 18, 2016, http://www.merriam-webster.com/dictionary/reject.

CONNECT WITH US!

(Spiritual Growth)

Facebook.com/CharismaHouse

@CharismaHouse

Instagram.com/CharismaHouseBooks

(Health)

Pinterest.com/CharismaHouse

(Fiction)

Facebook.com/RealmsFiction